Fake Christianity

C.B. MATTHEWS

WestBow
PRESS

A DIVISION OF THOMAS NELSON

WestBow Press books may be ordered through booksellers or by contacting:

WestBow Press
A Division of Thomas Nelson
1663 Liberty Drive
Bloomington, IN 47403
www.westbowpress.com
1-(866) 928-1240

Because of the dynamic nature of the Internet, any web addresses or links contained in this book may have changed since publication and may no longer be valid. The views expressed in this work are solely those of the author and do not necessarily reflect the views of the publisher, and the publisher hereby disclaims any responsibility for them.

Any people depicted in stock imagery provided by Thinkstock are models, and such images are being used for illustrative purposes only.

Certain stock imagery © Thinkstock.

ISBN: 978-1-4497-3692-7 (sc)
ISBN: 978-1-4497-3693-4 (hc)
ISBN: 978-1-4497-3691-0 (e)

Library of Congress Control Number: 2012900365

Printed in the United States of America

WestBow Press rev. date: 01/30/2012

Contents

Acknowledgments

I would like to thank my wife for the wonderful encouragement, challenging, love, and support she gave me throughout this entire process. Without you it would never have gotten finished, and I cannot express in words how much I appreciate all you do for me and our family on a daily basis. No husband has been more blessed and children have an example of what a truly Proverbs 31 woman is. We are so lucky to wake up every day and get to spend our lives with you in it.

I would also like to thank all the friends and family who showed love and support, and helped me persevere in finishing the book when I wanted to give up. Especially, Patrick and Amy C., Joanna R., and Jo C. who said that she would be the one person who read it, if no one else did.

Last, but certainly not least, I would like to thank God, Jesus Christ, and the Holy Spirit. If not for the leading, interceding, conviction, encouragement, love, and still small voice of reassurance from all three of you I would have never wrote one word of this. Praise and all glory to you, may your will be done, and please bless this feeble attempt by one of your servants.

Preface

I suppose starting at the beginning is always an intelligent idea. First, I would like to say that I am not writing this of my own accord. Feeling impressed by God for a long time to write a book, I am finally succumbing to the pressure. I have laid out a fleece too many times as Gideon did, only to have God prove Himself faithful again and again. It was when we reached a point where He started to reveal His frustration with me that I really got this flowing.

I've also had to overcome many temptations in this process. I threw many questions at God. "What if not one person ever reads this book?" I asked. To this He replied, "If one person reads it, would it not be worth it?" I conceded that He was right, after which He impressed upon me, "But even if no one ever reads it, you should write it because I am telling you to write it." I then questioned, "But why, God? Why, when there are so many good Christian writers out there and so many awesome Christian books in the bookstores? Can't people just read *those* books?" He answered, "So, what is one more?" Then, as I said, I would lay out fleece after fleece so God could prove to me one more time that I was supposed to do this.

One instance was pretty humorous; I remember praying and praying to God that He would show me beyond a shadow of a doubt that He wanted me to write a book. Then I put my Bible on the table and shut it. I prayed that He would somehow show me in Scripture that I was to be a writer. I thought that I had outsmarted Him; where in Scripture does it even talk about being a writer? The deal I made with Him was that I would open the Bible randomly and read the first verse that my eyes fell on. Much to my own horror, my eyes fell upon the end of Psalm 45:1, which in the NASB[1] reads, "My tongue is the pen of a ready writer." I got up and ran away from my Bible.

Even after that, I continued to question God and to lay out fleeces until, after the last fleece was answered, He impressed upon my heart that He had answered me enough times faithfully. I remember Him asking me very pointedly when I was going to start being faithful to Him—and to what I knew He had called me to do. Since I prided myself on being faithful and following God, that really hit me hard and started moving me in the right direction.

Unfortunately, a sad detour happened after that. I made the mistake of listening to other people's voices instead of God's. I went to my father, who is a good Christian man, and told him of my plans to write a book because I felt God leading me to do so. I was genuinely surprised and crushed at his reply: "Well, you can't make a living at that. Why would you want to do that?"

This caused doubt and confusion to enter my mind. For a long time I listened to these thoughts and gave in to the idea that surely my dad knew what he was talking about. I mean, why should I write a book? I was just a simple country boy who grew up on a farm. Even though I'd graduated from seminary, my master's degree was just in Marriage and Family Counseling, so what did I know about Christian living? What could I possibly write that anyone would want to read?

Furthermore, there were hundreds, if not thousands, of smarter, more educated people than I, who were better at English and could write better than I could.

So I listened to all of this, reasoning and justifying that God could not really want me to do such a thing. This resulted in not writing—and being perfectly happy about it—because when a whiff of the Holy Spirit

---

[1]   The Zondervan New American Standard Study Bible. Grand Rapids: Zondervan, 1999.

would come in and convict me for not writing, I would quickly crush it with the reasoning mentioned above.

To make a long story short, I half-did what God wanted me to do. I knew He wanted me in full-time ministry, and I knew he wanted me to write a book. So I surrendered to full-time ministry because I knew God would make me miserable if I did not at least listen to part of what He was calling me to do. I became the director of a campus ministry at a college, and He grew and stretched me in many areas (and is still doing so). Periodically, He would ask again, "What about the book?" And again I would ignore Him.

So I took on more and more responsibility. My wife and I were running two different youth groups and the college ministry, and I was filling in every Sunday at a very small church, where the congregation just wanted someone to preach to them. Four nights out of the week I was speaking and teaching God's word to people, and I couldn't have been happier. Then God started shouting in my quiet times that He still wanted me to write the book. So I did what may have been really dumb to do—in hindsight. I laid out the final fleece before I started writing these words you are reading today.

I asked God to make me miserable, because I was so blissfully happy in ministry life that I honestly thought there was no way I could be miserable. If God really wanted me to write, He would make me miserable, but there was no way that could happen . . . right?

There are no words that I could put on this page to share how utterly wrong I was. I became more miserable than I have ever been. I would preach or teach a wonderful lesson that God had laid on my heart, and people would respond to it. But then I would go home and cry. We would go on fun trips, like skiing with the youth or college students (and I *love* skiing), and I would get absolutely zero enjoyment from it. I considered checking myself into a mental institution or at least going to see a counselor. But God gently reminded me of my prayer and assured me that I wasn't losing my mind.

I prayed to God and told Him that I got it. I fully understood the lesson He was teaching me, and I asked Him to please take it away. He replied, "No, you don't. You haven't got it, and I'm not taking it away until you start writing." This led me to today. I have started writing, and I have many more stories to tell and will share them in this book, Lord willing. So now that you know a little of what got this book going, I think we can almost begin.

This book isn't meant to extensively cover the Christian life or how to live it in general. This is just one man listening to God and writing what the Lord has laid on his heart.

If you want to know how to live the Christian life, I would suggest reading your Bible daily, praying daily, and attending a church where they preach the Word and fear God. If you want to be able to follow God with strong and committed faith, then I would repeat the above instructions and advise you that it will not be all sunshine and puppies in your Christian life. The refining fire of God is intense and is no joking matter. Well, I think I am getting ahead of myself. Let's begin.

CHAPTER 1

Lies

The devil is a better theologian than any of us
and is a devil still.
—A. W. Tozer

One of my biggest pet peeves as a father is when my kids lie to me. I instantly turn from a nice, loving, understanding dad into a fire-breathing, steam-coming-out-my-ears, red-faced, yelling dad. Ashamedly, I usually go too far in berating them for the lie they either got by me, or tried to get by me.

This has recently resulted in my children turning into the Lie Police. They cannot wait until one of them lies, and then they will trample each other to get to daddy first and inform him of the lie. At church they get in other kids' faces and call them out on *their* lies. While I can be proud that they are dedicated to finding out lies and not lying, I wonder what kind of monstrosity I may be helping to create in them.

I get sick of my kids lying. I also get sick of lying to myself in my Christian life. When I reason or justify sin so I can do it more or feel better about myself, God is always faithful in my quiet time to show me just how disgusting those lies are.

That is why, when I look at the American church today and the majority of people who call themselves Christians, I feel nauseated. It is sickening, the lies that are being followed and swallowed in the church today. Whether they come from our culture, beliefs, sinful nature, or Satan himself, I don't know, and I really couldn't care less. All I know is that these lies are being consumed by the church, by whole denominations, and by unsuspecting Christians who should know better.

Lies come in all shapes and sizes. We are going to go over some of the ones that are the most obvious. You may or may not agree that these are lies, and that is okay. As my childhood pastor is so fond of saying, "You have the right to be wrong." I don't mind telling the truth or getting in people's faces with the truth. Why? Because God has not always been gentle with me in getting sin out of my life or smacking me upside the head when I am happily following a lie—which leads us to our first lie.

Lie #1:   *Since God is a loving and merciful God, He is always happy with me, no matter what I do.*

This lie I learned about the hard way, although it resulted in me giving my life to Christ wholeheartedly, so there was a happy ending. Regardless, I imagine I should give a bit of background before I get to it.

I grew up in a loving Christian home. My dad was a deacon and active member of the church. My mom played the piano and taught preschool classes for as long as anyone can remember. I was blessed enough to even have the same preacher my whole life, and he is still the pastor of that church today. He is a great Bible teacher and does not mind taking a stand on the Word. I was doubly blessed to grow up in a Christian family and be raised in a good church.

Yet, just like many other sinful and all-knowing teens in adolescence, I started to rebel. I ran after the desires of my own heart, because my parents and church family obviously didn't know anything and were keeping me from having real fun in life. This resulted in my partying with drinking and drugs, as well as chasing lustfully after any girl that paid attention to me. In summary, I was addicted to anything that gave me pleasure, and I didn't care what God or the Bible had to say about it.

To make matters worse, I still went to church during this time and played the part of a perfect Christian. Since I had a good upbringing, I answered all the questions correctly, sang songs when it was worship time, and listened to the preacher when I was not sleeping through the sermon. It went on this way with minimal conviction from God, because I would drown out His voice with partying and girls throughout the week and think about those things while in church when I wasn't playing the part of fake Christian. Things went along great until I decided to go on a mission trip to South Padre Island and participate in a ministry called "Beach Reach."

The main motivation behind going was that I was in college, it was Spring Break, and I had heard it was a great party scene. That's right: my inspiration to go on a mission trip was not to do work for God, honor Christ with my time, or witness to unbelievers. It was to see if the booze was free-flowing and the girls were hot. If anyone ever deserved to be struck dead by God nowadays, I would have been first in line.

I went, and it was everything I wished for. There were hot girls, people drinking, and drugs being passed around. Before I got to participate in the festivities, though, I had to attend our first worship service. At the beginning, there was a drama about a college student who was struggling with living out his faith. It was a silent drama played out to the song "Hanging by a Moment" by Lifehouse. The student finally decided to stop caring about what other people thought and to live out his faith. He witnessed to his friends, and it ended with some rejecting his message and others believing and receiving Christ as their Savior.

I was really touched by the drama, and then, while everyone was involved in worshipping God, He spoke to me.

It was one of the few times in my life that I felt like He audibly spoke in my mind. Ninety-nine percent of the time, God speaks to me in a still, small voice in my heart or in my mind—but I digress.

He was speaking loud and clear, and it was not what I expected to hear. He informed me that I was like that college student who cared too much about what other people thought. He told me that I was a worthless Christian and that all of my so called "friends" did not know Jesus Christ as their Savior. I was all too happy to not tell them about

Him, and so I was gladly endorsing them going to hell. God broke my heart when He told me he wanted me to stop being a useless Christian, to quit playing church and hurting the name of His Son by calling myself a Christian. He informed me that He wanted me to just leave the church, because I was doing nothing but mocking Him and His Word by the life I was living.

I broke down and wept like I have never cried in my life. While everyone else was singing a praise song to God, I was crying like a baby. While everyone else was feeling close to God, I had never felt farther away from Him. I was broken, and as I sat there in spiritual pieces, what hurt the most was that everything God had said was *true*. There were no spiritual painkillers to numb it away either.

As I sat there, I cried out to God that I didn't want to be that way anymore and that if He still loved me I would follow Him with all my heart. I told Him that for the first time in my life I truly wanted Jesus Christ to be my Lord and King and to have my whole life, that He could control my beliefs and have my thoughts, actions, and desires—I didn't want them anymore.

I have never felt so overwhelmed with love before, and that made me cry even harder. He impressed upon my heart that He did still love me, and that following Him was what He had wanted for me for such a long time. He accepted my cries of repentance and for forgiveness.

He also revealed that it wasn't going to be an easy road. I had many things in my life that I needed to stop doing or get rid of. One of the first things was to go to the party house where all my "friends" were and tell them what had happened on the mission trip. By God's grace and with the help of an awesome Christian girl who is now my wife, I was able to do it, but the results were not what I expected.

I went to the house with Bible in hand. While literally shaking, I told them about the trip and what had happened. Meanwhile, they looked at the Bible I was holding like it was a live snake. I had envisioned that some of them would listen and possibly convert. I had expected that, overall, it would be a great experience.

What really happened was far different. They all laughed at me. They made fun of me and reminded me of how much I liked to party. As I was leaving, they told me to my face that they would take bets on how long it would take before I was back there partying with them. My first obedient step of faith did not turn out as expected, but thanks to God, I was able to follow it. I believe that if I had not followed that first step, I would never have taken the other faith steps that have led me to today.

That is how I learned that God can actually be unhappy with the way I live. The sad thing is that there are a lot of Christians and many churches out there that paint the picture that God is happy with you no matter what. They teach and preach that God is only a loving God, always merciful and full of grace and forgiveness. He is those things, but He also has other attributes involving wrath, judgment, holiness, refinement, and discipline. People don't like to talk about those, though. They paint the picture of the Christian life as all sunshine and puppies— free from problem and hardships. By focusing only on God's love and mercy, we can always have a smile on our faces because God loves us. We never have to focus on sin, because God is happy, loving, and would never want us to feel bad. As one of my many favorite speakers, Voddie Baucham, likes to say, "Do you smell what I'm steppin' in?"

After giving a message on God's wrath, I've actually had people get in my face with tears streaming down their faces to yell at me. More people than I care to remember have gotten very mad when I've pointed out that God is not happy with sinners who are stuck in their sins and that He might actually be ready to punish or discipline them. One married couple took turns accosting me, and the wife kept asking me in an emotional, angry voice, "What about God's love? What about God's forgiveness?" They proceeded to berate me for having the nerve to focus on anything but the positives with Christians, because that is what we need to hear more about these days.

As I look around the church and Christians in general, I would have to firmly disagree. We have preachers who couldn't care less about what God really has to say to their churches. They care more about pleasing everyone and that the congregation goes home feeling good instead of being convicted of sin. Do they think that God is more interested in people feeling good in church rather than hearing His truth? I would hope they would take into consideration the fact that they should preach what God wants them to say, no matter what happens, but sadly there are too many Christians today that think no one should ever be offended in church. They believe that we should all be politically correct and never stand on absolutes in our faith. Have they forgotten that the third chapter of James claims that those who teach will be judged more strictly?

Oh, I'm sorry. I shouldn't have brought that up, because it will start a whole new firestorm. God is a God of judgment. Unfortunately, that is looked upon as heresy in many denominations today. How could a loving God, full of compassion and mercy, ever judge anyone? Where is the forgiveness? Again, I'm sorry, but it is written multiple times in the Old and New Testament that we will be judged for our actions, whether they were good or bad. I don't claim to know exactly how it is going to work, but I know that it scares me and motivates me to watch how I live, what I say, and what I do in this life.

We should be monumentally concerned with living our Christian lives in such a manner to receive a "Well done, good and faithful servant" when we go to heaven. That is another part of this lie that is bought into so quickly. I'm saved, so no matter what I do, I am good in God's eyes. Since God is so loving and nice, why would I not get a "Well done, good and faithful servant" when I get to heaven? Actually, I know how sinful I am, and I know how many times I intentionally thumb my nose at God and follow my own will for my life. I will be lucky to get a "well done" when I finally make it home.

So many Christians live in this fog of how great *they* are instead of how great *God* is, how lucky God is to have them on His team instead of how lucky we are to be loved by such an awesome God and how honored we should be that He would actually want to use depraved sinners such as us. They think that God is so happy with them because they tithe every paycheck, are involved in church activities, and listen to the sermons preached every Sunday—instead of giving to God their whole lives and letting Him be in charge.

This is easily seen in where their priorities are—and where yours are, for that matter. Are you more concerned with watching your nightly television shows instead of spending time with God or doing work for Him? Are you so wrapped up in life and everything that has to be done that you never have a family devotional with your family?

Do you ever spend time in God's word or in prayer to Him for more than just superficial reasons? Is His will and His way for your life more important than your will and your way? These are only a few of the important questions that need to be answered when examining your Christian life.

God is happy with you when you are seeking His will and His way for your life above all else. God is happy with you when you admit you are powerless against sin in your life without His help. God is happy with you when you turn from sin, ask for forgiveness, and try your hardest not to be involved in that sin again. Then, when you fail time and time again, you just keep repeating the process. God is happy when we as Christians take a stand on His word and do not back down to anyone. God is happy when we speak truth into the lives of unbelievers and believers alike, with no fear of political correctness or offense.

I hope that you can understand the idea that God is not happy with us when we do certain things in our Christian lives. When we run our lives according to our desires and our priorities, God is not happy with us. If we listen to the numerous lies of Satan and let that eventually render us ineffective Christians, God is not happy with us. The day we buy into the lie that, since we are saved and believe that Jesus Christ is our Savior, we have our golden ticket to heaven and can do whatever we want while never really letting Him become our Lord, King, Teacher, and Master . . . God is *not* pleased!

Are His grace, mercy, love, and forgiveness gone? No! Is He just waiting to crush us like a bug because we stepped out of line? By no means! He still loves us, but He is serious about us following Him, obeying Him, sacrificing for Him, desiring Him, and being involved in a relationship with Him. Do not think that He will not punish you, discipline you, or pull you aside and smack you upside the head. Why? Because He loves you. His love carries discipline, chastisement, and sometimes "getting in our face" because of how much He loves us. It isn't meant to drive us away, make us feel like giving up, or overwhelm us with feeling bad. It is meant to draw us closer, make us stronger, identify sin, and help us continue down the straight and narrow path.

Please do not buy into the lie that, whatever you do in life, God will be happy with you. Realize that God is a loving father who disciplines

His children. He is a holy God who is against sin, wherever it may be found. He does love you, and part of His love is to refine us to be more like Him, and that is rarely easy or gentle.

We will leave this subject with a verse through which I hope God reveals something to you.

"For in just a very little while, 'He who is coming will come and not delay. But my righteous one will live by faith. And if he shrinks back, I will not be pleased with him.' But we are not of those who shrink back and are destroyed, but of those who believe and are saved" (Hebrews 10:37-39).

Lie #2: Everyone is the same in God's eyes.

I have struggled mightily with how to word this lie. I pray that you hear the heart and theme of this lie. I considered saying, "God's love is for everyone," but I thought that would be too confusing, because God's love *is* for all people, whether they choose to accept it or reject it. I thought it could also be phrased, "God loves everyone the same," but again I thought too many people would get hung up on the wording. This resulted in a broader wording, and I feel comfortable that it is something upon which we can agree. I wanted to put a smiley face after the previous sentence, but that is probably not proper in writing. Know that I am smiling now. And now I want to write an lol (laugh out loud), but again it is not exactly proper in writing, so I will quit amusing myself so we can move on.

Is everyone the same in God's eyes? No. Does He view those who follow His word and His will for their lives in a different light? Yes. How do I say these things so confidently? Because of Scripture—period and end of story.

We need to base our thinking, feelings, and actions on God's holy, living Word. Like Ken Ham likes to say in his *Answers in Genesis* series, we need to put on our biblical glasses and see the world through a biblical worldview. We do not base our Christian thinking on anything else. Why? Because people will fail you, feelings change, and we do not believe just what sounds nice. When I say that God does view Christians differently and has serious expectations of you as a Christ-follower, I hope we can agree.

Let me talk for a little while to the three or four unbelievers who might actually read this, before we dive deeper into this lie. If you are not a follower or believer in Christ, then you probably disagree with me or think I am crazy. I am inclined to agree with you on the crazy part, but that would be a different subject entirely. Many people in your shoes, and in the church as well, believe many different things about God, but one of the common beliefs is that everyone is the same in God's eyes.

Does God love everyone? Yes. Does that mean everyone gets the same treatment when we die? No. There is a heaven for those who believe, and there is a hell for those who do not. God does not want you to go to hell, though. The last part of 2 Peter 3:9 reads, "He is patient with you, not wanting anyone to perish, but everyone to come to repentance." He has offered His hand of mercy and forgiveness through the sacrifice of Jesus Christ His one and only Son.

But why do you need a sacrifice or repentance? Romans 3:23 states, "For all have sinned and fall short of the glory of God." In this sense, everyone is the same; everyone on the face of this earth is a sinner. It has been that way since Adam and Eve first disobeyed and rebelled in the Garden of Eden. (That is a true, historical account that really happened—in case you think it is just a Bible story.) That is where sin entered the world, and we all suffer the effects from that. I am sorry if that challenges your sense of fairness, but oh,well—the truth hurts sometimes. There is hope, though; God would not leave you without a way out, with no way to salvation. Read Romans 5:12-21 for a better understanding, but a short summary is this: sin entered the world through one man (Adam), and it affects everyone for all time. But through the obedience of one man (Jesus Christ) and the grace of God, we have a gift of salvation that covers all sins. Through the sacrifice of Jesus Christ, all can have eternal life in heaven with God.

One of the most recognized verses of the Bible across the world, John 3:16, reads, "For God so loved the world that he gave his one and only Son, that whoever believes in him shall not perish but have eternal life."

The verses that follow give even more insight: "For God did not send His Son into the world to condemn the world, but to save the world through him. Whoever believes in him is not condemned, but whoever does not believe stands condemned already because he has not believed in the name of God's one and only son. This is the verdict: Light has come into the world, but men loved darkness instead of light because their deeds were evil" (John 3:17-19). One more important verse on salvation would be this one, Romans 10:9-10, which reads: "That if you confess with your mouth, "Jesus is Lord," and believe in your heart that God raised him from the dead, you will be saved. For it is with your heart that you believe and are justified, and it is with your mouth that you confess and are saved."

I urge you today to make the decision to accept God's gift of salvation through belief in His Son Jesus Christ. Make Him the Lord and King of your life, and start the journey today. Do not put it off. At the end of 2 Corinthians 6:2, it says, "I tell you, now is the time of God's favor, now is the day of salvation." Today is the day to give your life to the only living God, who loves you more than you can imagine.

You might be thinking, *Are you sure about this? What about all the other religions, or what about all the other questions I don't have answers for?* I know this: "Salvation is found in no one else, for there is no other name under heaven given to men by which we must be saved" (Acts 4:12). Believe in Him today, and He will change your life in ways that you would not and could not even imagine or believe, even if I told you.

You might ask, "What happens if I don't believe? What is the consequence? Is it hell?" *Yes!* It is eternal separation from God.

Luke 16:19-31 gives an example of what hell is like. It is a place where you are in eternal agony on many different levels.

1. You will be in physical agony from being alive in flames that never cease. It will be so bad that you will wish that someone would just dip their finger in water and let that drop on your tongue so you would just have a second of relief from the horrible pain.
2. You will be in emotional torment. Part of it will be from the realization that you were wrong about

a God who loved you more than you could ever comprehend, and part will be from the knowledge that you rejected that love and now are living in pain, forever separated from that love.

3. There will also be the worry and torment that comes from wishing you could go back and tell loved ones and relatives about Jesus Christ and the God whose love you rejected, because you would not want them to end up in the same place.

That kind of pain is unimaginable for me to even try to put into words. Needless to say, you don't want to end up there. Nobody does, and we should not wish it on anyone else either—not even the most evil men in the history of the world. Why? When we understand how horrible and unimaginable the endless torture and agony will be in hell, and when we know there is another place at the opposite end of the spectrum of unimaginable goodness, joy, peace, and rest where they *could* spend eternity—how could we wish hell upon anyone?

When we understand that everyone on the face of the earth deserves hell because we have sinned against a holy, righteous, and loving God but that there is salvation through Jesus Christ, it should make us realize how lucky we are to have such a gracious and forgiving God. Then we will recognize that we should be trying to save as many people as we can, whether they are good or bad people. It does not matter if you are a good or bad person; it matters what you believe, what you do with that belief, and what that belief does to you.

I hope you are seeing more clearly that everyone is not the same in God's eyes. There are those who believe and those who do not. There are those who are condemned, and those who are not. There are those who follow Him faithfully and those who do not. There are those who fear Him and those who do not. He looks upon these people differently; some receive His love and some do not. Some receive, grow from, and understand more of His love than others.

Let's look at some Scriptures that deal with these issues, since I can tell that some of you are about to explode after reading the previous paragraph. Psalm 103:11 reads, "For as high as the heavens are above the earth, so great is his love for those who fear him;" Does it say that so great is His love for *all*? Does it say that His great love is for *everyone*? No. But that is what you will hear from the world, from Satan, and even from people in church. (Now don't think that I am contradicting myself. We already went over how God's love is for everyone and how He doesn't want anyone to miss out on repentance but wants all to come to eternal life. Right now we are talking about the distinctions in His love for His people.)

Nobody wants to talk about this either, because they don't understand it, or it makes them uncomfortable. It is easier to hang out in the tent of "God loves everyone the same" or in the lie of "Everyone is the same in God's eyes." The verse refers specifically to those who fear Him. This is not a terror-fear or a state of being scared of him because He is so scary. The fear this is talking about is a respectful fear. It is an awe of God that motivates you to obey His commandments and follow Him in your life through obedience and faithfulness. It is being afraid of His punishment and discipline, but it is not a cowering fear that can incapacitate us. It is more like your fear of a good parent when you were a child; you knew beyond a shadow of a doubt that they loved you, but you also knew that if they discovered that you were doing something bad, you were going to get punished or disciplined. That is how the fear of God should work in us. Psalm 103:17-18 explains, "But from everlasting to everlasting the Lord's love is with those who fear him, and his righteousness with their children's children—with those who keep his covenant and remember to obey his precepts."

This begs the question: what happens to—or how does God view—the people who do not fear Him, keep His covenant, or remember to obey His precepts? The answer is complex and simple at the same time. (That seems to happen a lot when we are talking about different aspects of the Christian life.) God does view in a negative light those people who do not fear Him, who forsake His covenant, and who forget to obey His precepts. Like any good father, He is not pleased with disobedient, disrespectful, and uncaring children. It doesn't mean that you are not loved; it means that you are loved completely, since you have a father who will discipline you when you get out of line. This is so you will know the difference between right and wrong, so you will grow up and not remain a baby, and so you will learn to trust Him at His Word.

What happens to you as a Christian when you do not fear Him, keep His covenant, or remember to obey His precepts? You are setting yourself up to get in trouble on many levels.

YOU ARE IN DANGER OF GETTING DISCIPLINED BY A LOVING FATHER.

My parents spanked me, and it was okay. I look back and thank God that I was spanked as a child and that I feared that punishment; it kept me out of some trouble, but not all. I also knew that for every time I was ever spanked unfairly, there were a hundred times when I did not get spanked when I deserved it, so it was okay.

My dad even carved out a board with my name on one side and my brother's on the other. One time as I was bending over to receive a spanking, I saw that my dad was going to spank me with my brother's side. After I received the spanking, I was all too happy to share with him—in a snippy tone—how wrong he was to spank me with my brother's side. I learned very quickly just how dumb that was. He informed me that he could fix the situation with one spank—by using the correct the side of the board, and a second spank to correct me for talking disrespectfully to him. Looking back now, it is funny how we act as children, although it isn't funny or without pain at the time.

I believe we need to look at God's discipline in this way. God disciplines us because He loves us. His discipline does not feel good at the time, but if we let it do what it is supposed to, amazing things can happen. We will grow in our Christian faith, beliefs, strength, knowledge, convictions, etc. If we complain about getting punished, we must ask why we are getting punished. And if we get snippy with God while getting punished, we shouldn't be surprised if we get punished or disciplined more—or if God says tough things or asks tough things of us in response to our snippyness, or if we feel sheepish for questioning God at all.

Let me reiterate that discipline does not feel good; it isn't meant to. It is awesome, though, that instead of discipline God often overwhelms us with love, grace, and mercy. In my experience, He also is great about giving multiple second chances before He pours out His discipline. If you are getting disciplined or punished by God, remember that it is because He loves you, and He only wants what is best for you. That alone should bring some comfort and assurance to your soul.

You are in danger of weakening, damaging, or deliberately choosing to forsake your Christian faith or walk when you do not fear Him, keep His covenant, or forget to obey His precepts.

When we do not fear Him, we begin to think about God in ways that He is not. We think that He is all love, so we act any way we want to and think it's okay. This results in not living for God the way we are supposed to. We don't have to sacrifice anything for God because He is always patting us on the head, telling us how good we are. We don't care about sin in our lives, because God is happy with us just the way we are. We can live for ourselves and do anything we want, because God just wants us to be happy in this life. This will lead us down the path of not caring about what God thinks, because we feel that He doesn't care about us. This can all come from not fearing the Lord, and I hope you can see how dangerous this lie is.

When we do not keep His covenant or maintain our relationship with Him, we very easily slip into faithless lives. If we start to forsake His covenant, His promises, or our relationship with Him, it takes us down a faith-killing path. When you become faithless in one area of your Christian life, it very easily spreads to others. We don't even realize it at times. We stop praying to God, and next we have stopped reading our Bibles and having quiet times with God. Then we move on to losing interest in church activities; we see no real value in them, because we have already drifted away from God and our personal relationship with Him. So then we stop going to church because of whatever foolish excuse we want to come up with, and before we know it, we are questioning the very foundations of our faith.

Hopefully, it is then that we have a come-to-Jesus moment. Sadly, though, that is when many former Christians and kids raised in Christian homes will walk away from the faith for a long time—or forever. All of this stems from not remaining faithful to God. Remember, *He* never stops being faithful; *we* are the ones who do a great job of being faithless in our Christian lives.

YOU ARE IN DANGER OF FORGETTING TO OBEY HIS PRECEPTS, WHICH LEADS TO DISOBEDIENCE, AND DISOBEDIENCE LEADS TO A CONTAMINATED CHRISTIAN LIFE.

Galatians 6:7 says, "Do not be deceived: God cannot be mocked. A man reaps what he sows."

If you sow disobedience, do not be surprised when you start to hate the Word of God, church activities, or the influence of the Holy Spirit. This all comes from forgetting or intentionally rebelling against God and His precepts.

Forgetting can be a complex issue.

We forget because we are human and are just not thinking at the moment. We can more easily forget when we are tired, overwhelmed, or just busy with too many things. It can be easy to intentionally rebel or sin and then excuse it away under the guise of forgetfulness. We can also forget because we just don't care anymore. This is a sad testament to our relationship to God, if we are forgetting because of a loss of relationship with Him.

Forgetting also implies that, once upon a time, there was prior knowledge to be forgotten. When I look around today at Christianity in general, I see that Christians have not always forgotten to obey God's precepts; sometimes they do not know His precepts at all. Why? That in itself could be a three-hundred-page answer, but here are just a few.

While there are Christian churches today that don't teach the Bible because it is an antiquated book that does not fit our culture, *Christians will not know God's precepts!*

When denominations that used to be Christian and held the Bible up as their belief system start cutting out passages of God's Word that are not politically correct, that make people feel uncomfortable, or that are too convicting, *Christians will know nothing of God's precepts!*

When pastors do not stress the infallibility of God's Word, compromise the Word for any reason, and preach sermons from secular authors instead of the Bible, *Christians will not know God's precepts!*

Why stress this point? Because it seems that more and more frequently we have to deal with children who grew up in Christian homes but walk away from the faith when they leave home. More and more often, there are "Christians" accepting sin in their lives—sin that the Bible says is completely wrong—but these "believers" couldn't care less what the Bible says about it. We have millions of Christians running to empty wells of drugs, alcoholism, pornography, materialism, ungodly relationships—or just fill in the blank with whatever sin-trap has captured them.

There are millions of Christians who know just the bare minimum, who do not want to know any more, because at least they are saved. Why should they learn any more when they already have a loving God and eternal bliss? What more could God want of them?

I hope you are beginning to see or already know that He wants a lot more. He wants to be the Lord and King of your life, and that encompasses all areas.

Christianity and the church today are full of believers to whom the author of Hebrews was referring in Hebrews 5:11-14:

> We have much to say about this, but it is hard to explain because you are slow to learn. In fact, though by this time you ought to be teachers, you need someone to teach you the elementary truths of God's word all over again. You need milk, not solid food! Anyone who lives on milk, being still an infant, is not acquainted with the teaching about righteousness. But solid food is for the mature, who by constant use have trained themselves to distinguish good from evil.

This should strike deep into our hearts if we are guilty of being happy to stay in the infancy stage of our Christian lives. Some of you reading this book are called to do something more than just go to church and get fed all the time. There are some of you that are called to be teachers, pastors, missionaries, and worship leaders—or whatever God has called or is going to call you to do. This will stretch and test you in ways that you cannot imagine. It will take growing up, and you will go through growing pains. It will not be easy; it will not always be peace-filled; you will not always enjoy doing God's work. But it will be the most rewarding and maturing aspect of your Christian life. I know that I want to be able to "distinguish good from evil" and not fall prey to my sinful nature or Satan's lies. I hope you do as well.

It is amazing how the lie, *"Everyone is the same in God's eyes,"* could go down so many paths. This is the way of Satan and our sinful nature. One lie can present itself in many ways that are more complex than what we give them credit for or see at first glance. If you believe part of a lie, or give it any value, it will then spread and infect your thinking, beliefs, and actions. You will get so far away from the truth that it can be a hard journey back.

Why not just believe God and His Word at face value? When God says something is wrong or is a lie, we need to believe that above all else. We need to hold fast to the truth no matter how our thinking, feelings, or actions want to sway us the wrong way.

In closing out this chapter, let us review how everyone is not the same in God's eyes. There are righteous and unrighteous. There are mature believers and immature believers. Some believers fear God, and some do not. There are those who keep His covenant and those who do not. There are those who obey His precepts and those who do not, and there are some who forget to obey.

There are people in this world who choose to believe in Jesus Christ as the Savior of the world, and there are many who do not.

Some people sow and then reap good, righteous aspects in their lives, and others sow and then reap destructive, evil aspects. Everyone is offered grace, mercy, and salvation, but not everyone will choose to believe or follow it.

There will be those who will receive no eternal condemnation at the judgment in the afterlife, and there will be those who receive eternal condemnation at the judgment.

Some parents teach their children God's precepts and raise them up in righteous households, and some *never* teach them God's precepts in their home or in their lives, thinking that it is the church's job to do so.

You can see how this could go on and on if we really wanted to take a step back and analyze how differently God sees people—those upon whom His favor rests and those on whom it does not.

Have some of these written words hit you hard? Do you find yourself identifying with falling prey to some of these lies?

You can do one of two things.

You can get mad, sad, or any other emotion that leads to you rejecting what has been said. You can then go back to your lukewarm or non-existent "Christian" life with a smile on your face because of how wrong the author was. You can tell all your friends about reading this particular book on Christian living and about how crazy it was and that it doesn't take believing in all that or living like that to be a good Christian.

Or you can let God take control. Let His Holy Spirit come in and convict, impress truth, or do anything else that has to be done. You can start reading your Bible every day to draw closer to God, let His living Word speak into your life, and learn what God's precepts are. Don't take my word for it—or that of any preacher or even family members, at times. God will reveal the most, teach the best, encourage, strengthen, motivate, and convict when you are diving into God's Word yourself. (Please don't think I'm saying not to listen to this book, your preacher, or godly family members. It is just more personal and helpful in your personal relationship with God when you read the Bible yourself.)

Take heart, Christian brother or sister, and be on guard for lies that will inevitably try to make their way into your Christian life.

CHAPTER 2

Beliefs

I would recommend that you either believe God up to
the hilt, or else not to believe at all. Believe this book
of God, every letter of it, or else reject it. There is no
logical standing place between the two. Be satisfied
with nothing less than a faith that swims in the deeps
of divine revelation; a faith that paddles about the edge
of the water is poor faith at best. It is little better than a
dry-land faith, and is not good for much.
—C. H. Spurgeon

What we believe is important. It shapes our thinking, feelings, and
actions. It motivates us to do things we would not normally do. It
comforts the soul in times of trouble. Our beliefs do much more than
this as well, so why do we as Christians live at times as if what we
believe is not really that important?

I can hear the cries now of, "Wait! What are you talking about?
I believe in God, and I believe in Jesus Christ as my Savior. Isn't that
enough?"

Can I say yes *and* no?

The fact that you believe in the one true, living God of the Bible
and that his Son is the only Savior of the world is the most important
belief you need to have. But to think that this is the *only* belief that

needs to be engraved upon your heart, soul, and mind for a genuine and authentic Christian life to flourish is just not right.

How will you get through life-shattering moments such as the death of a family member or special loved one, personal injuries that change everything, and other tragic moments that leave us dumbfounded, crushed, or broken? Where and what will you draw from to build a firm and steadfast faith?

It will take a belief system that can stand in these times and leave us with hope and assurance, even when we don't understand everything.

The beliefs discussed below are *not* an exhaustive list of beliefs we need to have as Christians. There are probably many more that we need to bring inside our Christian belief system. Also, I do not doubt that there are many more highly educated individuals who could write on this subject—and on all the topics covered in this book, for that matter—more extensively and more clearly than I can. These beliefs are just the ones that God has impressed upon me to share with you.

God Is In Control

He is in control, and He knows what He is doing. Our intelligence does not even compare to His, so quit trying to figure out everything that is going on! Just have faith and follow Him.

We need to rest in the fact that He is in control—and stop trying to wrest control back from Him. When we give God control of our lives, it takes a burden off of us. It will reduce our stress level. We might worry about new things when He starts to reveal His plan for our lives, but He doesn't want us to worry. Just know that He is in control.

What breaks my heart is looking around at Christianity in general and seeing that no one wants to give Him control. There is a diseased thinking that says we can be in control of our own lives and follow our own desires and plans for this fragile life and that God is okay with it. After all, why would God want me to do something that sounds crazy? Why would God give me desires to do something other than what He would really want me to do?

I will answer that with another question: Are those desires you speak of really from God? If they are desires that are only fueled by wanting to make lots of money, I would beg you to consider that they are not from God.

Are those desires fueled by doing only what makes you happy? I would beg you to let God decide what makes you happy.

Are those desires fueled by what you are good at? I would beg you to listen to God and see what He wants you to do with your life—instead of listening to a sin-filled world with sin-filled minds telling you what your sin-filled heart wants to listen to.

As an American Christian, I live in a culture that is *me-first.* Everything is focused on the individual. We see commercials around-the-clock about how to make our lives better by buying certain things. We are pressured to "rock the vote," because our vote matters. *Me, me, me* and *I, I, I* permeate our thinking to the point where we lose sight of how to function as part of a whole. We lose our ability to function in relationships, because they are all about *me.* And yet we wonder why the divorce rate is so high. We cannot function as part of the body of Christ, because we want either to be the whole body, or we want to pick which body part we are going to be. As a genuine Christian, the *me-first* belief system has to die.

When God is in control, we are His servants! When He is our Lord and King, we are supposed to be His loyal, faithful, and obedient subjects. If He is in control, we don't have a say in what we do in this life, nor do we get a vote; we do what He wants us to do. As Christians, we need to kill the belief that we can be in control of our lives. The words of Jesus found in Mark 8:34 state, *"If anyone would come after me, he must deny himself and take up his cross and follow me."*

What part of that verse reads, "Give in to every desire and pleasure that comes across your path because you want it"? No, it says "deny himself," so get used to denying yourself in the Christian life. We are not missing out when we deny ourselves. We are learning how to sacrifice, which comes in useful in this temptation-filled world. *Denial* has a negative connotation in our country, but it is not negative to God.

Where in the verse does it say to put down the cross you're bearing? Where in the verse does it say never to pick up a cross? I ask these questions because this is where a major portion of Fake Christianity, USA, walks with God.

Warning: sarcasm ahead!

God must have got it wrong in giving you your cross; He didn't know that it was so heavy. He is sorry; He didn't know it would be so hard for you. Oh, God is so sorry; the almighty King of Creation must have made a mistake when calling you into whatever job He wanted you to do because, from your perspective, that job is completely wrong for you.

No! In this verse we are called to *"take up your cross."* It does not matter how big, long, or heavy you think it will be. I'll let you in on a little secret. It will be as light as a feather when you follow Jesus with the right beliefs. It will be the heaviest and toughest challenge imaginable if you cling to sin-filled, selfish, unbiblical beliefs when trying to take up your cross.

Luke 9:23 mentions that we are to carry our cross "daily." This means that we are to be faithful in carrying our cross. It does not mean that we get to rest whenever we want to, just because we think we need a day off.

We follow and take up our cross, through the rain or the sunshine, when it is hot or cold, when it is uphill or downhill, when it is easy or hard, when it causes pain or when it is a joy, when we can see clearly by the light of the sun or when we cannot see because darkness is all around us.

If God is in control of your life, those previous sentences might bring a smile to your heart. However, if He is not, those sentences will either strike fear into your heart, convict you, or motivate you to actually try to live like that.

The hard thing is to really believe that you can. Until you actually start living in the realm of carrying your cross daily, you will be stuck in the I-don't-think-I-can-do-this line of thinking, because it is too hard, scary, or whatever else you think about it. You need to start living in the *I-can* line of thinking and actually take up your cross and follow Jesus to whatever end. In doing so, you will move from "I don't think I can do this" to "Praise God, I am actually living these things out. Wow! I never thought I could do that!" I hope that resonates with you.

There is a deep importance to the belief that God is in control. It will spread like a wildfire once you actually start believing, following, and living as if God is in control of your life. It will not be easy. Let me repeat that by saying, *It will be one of the hardest things you have ever done.* To give God control is to fly in the face of the world's thinking, desires, and wants for your life. Satan will bring a battalion with him to try to stop you from giving control to God. Always remember that God is bigger, stronger, and more important than anything that this world or Satan has to offer.

So, who are you going to give control to in this life? God, Satan, this world, or your sinful nature? Notice that there is only one right choice, while there are many wrong choices.

I pray that you will take a step of faith toward giving God control today.

GOD HAS A SPECIFIC PLAN FOR YOUR LIFE

It brings me comfort to know that. It should bring all Christians meaning and purpose in this life. To believe and know that God has you here for a reason and has tangible, specific things he wants you to do in your short time here on earth will help you accomplish many things in your Christian life.

One aspect this belief should accomplish in your Christian life is a sense of being *secure.* This security is a steadfastness of the soul. It's when the storm is raging around you or it's the night before you are to be executed—*and you are able to sleep.* Just like Jesus when he was with the disciples in the midst of a raging storm, and like Peter the night before he was to be executed, we need to have the calmness, peace, trust, and security to be able to sleep in a time like that. This is more than an attitude or feeling. It is resting in the fact that God is in control and that He has a plan for my life; I am not worried about what is going to happen because *whatever* happens to me or is happening around me does not matter.

As Christians we do not lose our faith, go crazy, or run around like chickens with our heads cut off when things happen to us that we do not understand or like or could even have imagined. We remain steadfast and secure in God's love for us. It may be part of His plan for unexplainable things to happen to us, and we need to be okay with that.

If tragedy strikes, don't get stuck on the *why*. Take a step back and consider a few things. Is it just the result of living in a fallen and sin-filled world? Is it a result of my own sin, something I actually have a part in, something that I need to repent of, something that carries lifelong consequences?

When we take the *why* question away and replace it with the God who has a plan for my life, better questions and perspective emerge: *What do you want me to learn from this God? Did You let this happen for a reason that is bigger than I can understand right now?* When we take time to answer some of these questions, we will get past the temptation to lose trust in God, lose faith in everything, blame God, or any number of sinful things that either we ourselves turn to or Satan himself is trying lead us into. *Our security in God needs to transcend everything we can or will turn to in this life.*

When you know, believe, and live out the fact that God has a plan for your life, it will give you the confidence and determination to do anything.

Many parents repeatedly tell their children as they are growing up, "You can do anything." I see how good this statement can be if you add, "that God wants you to do." But by itself, the statement "You can do anything" could be a great evil.

Why? Because our individualistic culture encourages materialism and living only for ourselves. It should not surprise us that the majority of Christian homes are turning out children that are only following worldly pursuits, when they should be turning out children who believe that God has a plan for their lives.

Presently, I am the director of a college campus ministry on a very secular Colorado campus. I am sick and tired of constantly trying to change the thinking of the "Christian" college student. Their priorities include: having the most fun they can have; getting involved in campus activities that interest them or bring them pleasure, status, or prestige; and finding a major that will make them the most money or bring them the most happiness in life.

When I challenge them to rearrange their priorities to include putting God first in their lives, spending time in activities that either glorify God or draw them closer to Him, and picking any major in college as long as they have cleared it with God first, I get some crazy looks, ignorant feedback, and hostile resistance.

These priorities should have been taught in the home by loving Christian parents, but it is obvious that they were not—or the student is just choosing to reject those lines of thinking at the present time.

College students and Christians in general need to know that they "can do anything." They can be a doctor, even when they do not think they are smart enough. They can be a politician or even the president of the United States, even when they are convinced that they can't lead or don't have good public-speaking ability. (Inside information on me: sometimes I speak up to four times a week, and I still feel like throwing up or shaking apart from nervousness, but God gets me through and will get you through as well, when you depend on Him.) Everything hinges on God leading you down these paths. Even if you have good intentions and plans that would all glorify God, if God has not planned that particular path for your life, *then do not do it!*

If you do not know what God wants you to do in your life, then just ask Him. He will answer you. He may answer with the job you will have for the rest of your life. He may reveal it just one faith-step at a time, where you have to follow Him in faith in order to get to the place where he will show you the next step you need to take. Just trust, obey, and step out in faith, *following His leading and His alone.*

I can hear the cries of, "I *have* asked, and He just has not answered!" Well, back up a minute and answer some questions first.

How Long Have You Asked?

Was it just in passing? Did you ask God while clinging to your own desires and plans for your life? It may take longer than you think for God to answer you. We are supposed to seek Him above all things. We are supposed to be patient and wait on God. If we are still clinging to our own desires, passions, and plans for our lives, *we will never truly listen for His answer.* Also, if we are not serious, have false intentions, or are frivolous with God in our asking, it makes me wonder why God should be serious or take the time to answer us.

WILL YOU ACCEPT HIS ANSWER?

This question applies to any job, not just a ministry job. If He answers that you need to surrender to the call of ministry and become a pastor, missionary, etc., will you accept it? Or do you instantly reject His answer, providing Him with a twenty-page answer, specifying why you could never do a job like that or be qualified for it? Fight the fear and trembling that will try to overwhelm you. Accept His answer; be comforted knowing that your King, Lord, and Savior has a plan for your life. He will be with you as you go on this journey. He will equip, correct, refine, and sustain you. But you will never experience any of this if you do not accept what His sovereign will is for your life. Believe that He is in control and knows what He is doing. Accept His answer, because you do not live for yourself anymore; you live for Him alone. "And he died for all, that those who live *should no longer live for themselves but for him* who died for them and was raised again" (2 Corinthians 5:15, emphasis mine).

The next question that usually comes up in this discussion deals with the *how.*

HOW DO YOU KNOW WHAT GOD'S WILL OR PLAN IS FOR YOUR LIFE?

The first part of the answer is to actually believe that you *can* know what God's will and plan is for your life.

At a retreat where I was leading a workshop on finding God's will for your life, one student was absolutely sure—and tried to convince everyone else—that God's will is like an "enigma." He went on to say that we could never really know what it is, that we can never really put our finger on it.

This is a sad line of thinking for any Christian. If we believe that God's will or plan for our lives is unknowable, then we are free to live whatever way we want. When I brought that point up to the student, I remember him saying, "No, that's not what I meant; I still want to do what God wants me to do."

"But how will you ever know if what you are doing is right and pleasing in God's eyes if you cannot know what He wants you to do—because it is some mysterious enigma?" I countered.

He was angry, then embarrassed, and finally conceded with, "Good point."

I asked, "So, do you think we can know what God's will is for our lives?"

He smiled and said, "I guess we'd better."

The Old and New Testaments give us many different examples of how people followed God's will for their lives. Some followed God faithfully, while others rejected His leading. There were severe consequences at times when individuals—or Israel as a nation—did not follow God's will. There were awesome rewards for those who persevered and did God's will, even amidst tribulation and sin in their lives. *Following God's plan cost many individuals their very lives.*

We need to understand that following God's will and plan for our lives is different for everyone. While all Christians should believe the same basic aspects of faith, this does not mean that every Christian life will be the same. Some of us will die for our faith, while others will live fulfilled lives with few or no problems.

There will be some Christians who work very hard and pour out their lives doing God's work, seeing no fruits or results from their work, while others will reap an abundant harvest off of others' work. This does not exactly make sense or even seem fair at times.

This is how God works, though, and this is how Scripture explains to us how it will be. We do not need to grow angry, sad, mad, or discouraged or give in to any other negative emotions, thoughts, or behaviors. Just resolve to do what God wants you to do in your life, and know that the results are in *His* hands.

Read the book of Ecclesiastes for a better understanding of what is meaningless in life and what is important. The ending of Ecclesiastes reverberates through the whole Bible and is something we need always to have in the back of our mind as affecting everything we believe in.

"Now all has been heard; here is the conclusion of the matter: Fear God and keep his commandments, for this is the whole duty of man.

For God will bring every deed into judgment, including every hidden thing, whether it is good or evil" (Ecclesiastes 12:13-14).

Before we leave the subject of believing God's plan and will for your life, we should go over some general aspects—and then some specific ones—on this topic.

GENERAL ASPECTS THAT ARE GOD'S WILL FOR EVERY CHRISTIAN

SANCTIFICATION

Simply stated, sanctification is the process of becoming increasingly more holy and righteous while here on earth. We become more and more godly in our beliefs, thinking, feelings, and actions. It doesn't stop until we die and become transformed into what we will be in heaven.

Here are some verses about sanctification in Romans 12:1-2: "Therefore, I urge you, brothers, in view of God's mercy, to offer your bodies as living sacrifices, holy and pleasing to God—this is your spiritual act of worship. Do not conform any longer to the pattern of this world, but be transformed by the renewing of your mind. Then you will be able to test and approve what God's will is—his good, pleasing and perfect will."

We can see from these verses that *non-conformation to the world*, *transformation*, and *renewal* are part of God's will for Christians. Understand that this is part of the sanctification process. Ephesians 5:15-20 says, "Be very careful, then, how you live—not as unwise but as wise, making the most of every opportunity, because the days are evil. Therefore do not be foolish, but understand what the Lord's will is. Do not get drunk on wine, which leads to debauchery. Instead, be filled with the Spirit. Speak to one another with psalms, hymns and spiritual songs. Sing and make music in your heart to the Lord, always giving thanks to God the Father for everything, in the name of our Lord Jesus Christ."

This passage implores Christians to not waste any time and to make the most of every opportunity. God's will for all of us is to not be foolish. We need to be defined by wise living; it is part of God's sanctification process.

Of course, we are going to mess up, but as we grow and mature in Christ, they should not be the same sins over and over. We need to have some victories in life over those sins. We should not fall into traps of sin and temptation regularly. Being filled with the Holy Spirit will help us with the defeat of sin, with the way we live, and with the kind of witness we have.

Do you speak to other Christians with joy coming out of your heart and soul? Do you encourage others by having conversations filled with psalms, hymns, and other spiritual songs? Or are all your conversations about how gloomy life is and how many problems you have, focusing primarily on the negatives in this life, with only a superficial shout-out to God tied on at the end? You are either becoming more sanctified or you are not. It is as simple as that.

> Finally, brothers, we instructed you how to live in order to please God, as in fact you are living. Now we ask you and urge you in the Lord Jesus to do this more and more. For you know what instructions we gave you by the authority of the Lord Jesus. It is God's will that you should be sanctified: that you should avoid sexual immorality; that each of you should learn how to control his own body in a way that is holy and honorable, not in passionate lust like the heathen, who do not know God; and that in this matter no one should wrong his brother or take advantage of him. The Lord will punish men for all such sins, as we have already told you and warned you. For God did not call us to be impure, but to live a holy life. Therefore, he who rejects this instruction does not reject man but God, who gives you his Holy Spirit." (1 Thessalonians 4:1-8)

In this passage we see a word-for-word description of what God's will is for the Christian in the sanctification process. Every Christian needs to avoid sexual immorality and impurity. All Christians need to learn how to control their bodies so they are not controlled by lust and temptations.

God called us to live holy lives. *It is something we are capable of doing.*

If you feel you are not strong enough to do this, that is okay. Cry out to God in fervent prayer, and ask Him to take away the desire to do these things; He will answer you. Get rid of anything in your home that tempts you or is a vessel to commit such sins. Get *Christian* counsel to help you deal with these things. The simplest way to word it is this: *Stop doing sexually immoral and impure things!* Take it minute by minute, hour by hour, or day by day, if need be. Fight against it like you have never fought before, and eventually you will see victory in these areas.

I am very passionate about this aspect of sanctification, because it is so personal to me. I let lust consume me at a very young age; it involved pornographic magazines and videos, looking for parts of the female anatomy that would arouse me, spending a lot of time fantasizing about doing sexual things with girls, and finally acting out on those impulses.

All those aspects resulted in my body, mind, and soul being controlled by lust like a depraved heathen. Looking back, it is no surprise that I ended up having pre-marital relations with girls and one of them producing a child outside of marriage.

It has been an uphill battle for the last decade of my life. Because I let myself be controlled by lust for approximately ten years during my adolescence and young adulthood, it did not just switch off when I gave my life to Christ. I had to learn through many mistakes and victories how to control my body.

All the details would fill up many pages, but I will just hit some of the general points I learned.

I could pray that God would take away my desire to commit these sins, and He would. But it was up to me to kill the temptations to commit such sins when they came back. I had to learn to stop fantasizing about women right at the beginning of when I would start fantasizing. I had to learn to control my eyes to not look at every beautiful woman that crossed my path in a lust-filled and unbiblical way. I found out that singing a hymn or praise song, telling God that He had made a beautiful creation, or immediately starting to pray about anything would help kill the lust in my heart. If you try these things or other means that God impresses upon your heart, I know you will find some victory. Just do not keep running back into the sin of lust, never taking any measures to change, and then blame God for not helping you. It is your choice whether or not you take this issue seriously in your life and *do* something about it.

Here's my last thought on this subject, I promise. One of the most influential aspects that has helped me monumentally in the struggle against lust was telling my wife about it. I will caution that this might need to be done with a pastor or Christian counselor present because of the reactions that may follow.

In the counseling program at seminary, they put you through a semester where you receive counseling before you can counsel anyone else. I remember the counselor telling us to bring something real to the counseling sessions, because we would not get much out of it if we just brought a fake problem or something that was not genuinely a problem for us.

So, I decided to take him at his word and bring something that had troubled and controlled me for the majority of my life. It was amazing to work on—until he informed me that I should tell my wife about it.

To make a long story short, I finally did. Through tears, pain, and just being blessed with an awesome, wonderful wife, there has been much victory in my life over lust. It is awesome that she has decided to stand beside me and help me fight the battle instead of blaming me, remaining hurt, or reacting or treating me in any number of other ways.

Just knowing now that I have to tell her if I view a pornographic image or movie on TV, on the Internet, or in a magazine helps immensely. Instead of keeping it a secret, I have an accountability partner. Knowing that if I mess up and have to tell her and see the pain, hurt, and tears in her eyes because of what I did—just because I could not control my own body—is enough to detour me from going down that road.

Does it mean that I am perfect? Of course not! But does it mean that I haven't viewed those kinds of materials in a long time? Yes! And once upon a time, I would have thought that to be impossible.

Back to more of God's will for every Christian: "Be joyful always; pray continually; give thanks in all circumstances, for this is God's will for you in Christ Jesus" (1 Thessalonians 5:16-18).

In this passage we see a little repeat of the Ephesians 5 passage (and a lot of the books of the Bible for that matter), although the verse is more specific here. God's will for every Christian is to have a life filled with rejoicing and being joyful, constantly being in communication with God through continual prayer and being someone who can give thanks in all circumstances. *This is part of the sanctification process.*

It is hard to be "joyful always" in such a sin-filled world, but we are supposed to believe it and then follow it up with a joy-filled life.

It is hard to be in constant communication with God if all you care about are your own desires, passions, plans, and worries in your life. Simply put, it is hard to pray if you only focus on yourself all the time.

It takes another level of faith and understanding to be thankful in all circumstances. We need to give thanks to God when we are hurting or in pain, not just when we are happy or feel that God is close. The verse says "in all circumstances," and that means *all*, folks—not just in circumstances where giving thanks comes naturally. It will take your faith and Christian life to a whole new level when you start thanking God within every circumstance that comes up in your life.

As you can see, sanctification is something that will turn your Christian life upside-down.

Will you start living and believing in a way where God can begin to sanctify you?

SECURITY

I know we have already hit on the importance of security a little bit, but some things can never be stressed too much. This kind of security is that of being secure in your knowledge that God is with you and cares for you, and that He will never let you down. He is worthy of all your faith, hope, and trust in Him. The next step is living out this newfound security through your thoughts, feelings, and actions. It will be a drastic change but a needed one if you are going to follow God's will and grow more in the process of sanctification.

Here are some verses about *security*:

Who shall separate us from the love of Christ? Shall trouble or hardship or persecution or famine or nakedness or danger or sword? As it is written: "For your sake we face death all day long; we are considered as sheep to be slaughtered." No, in all these things we are more than conquerors through him who loved us. For I am convinced that neither death nor life, neither angels nor demons, neither the present nor the future, nor any powers, neither height nor depth, nor anything else in all creation, will be able to separate us from the love of God that is in Christ Jesus our Lord." (Romans 8:35-39)

What a beautiful passage—one that all Christians need to hold on to in times of doubt, unbelief, and trouble, times when questions go unanswered or we feel alone. *It is part of God's will and plan for your life to be firmly secure in your Christian faith.*

How do we get to that point, though?

We read our Bibles, we pray to God, we memorize Scripture, and we have a quiet time with God. These times can be worshipful, times spent waiting on God to answer questions or just listening for His voice to impress something on our hearts and minds.

Why do we need to grow in biblical knowledge, faith, and understanding? So we will not be deceived.

So many Christians today are being deceived by philosophy, psychology, science, and any teacher under the sun that say things that make them feel good or "make sense" to them. These deceived Christians fail to recognize that they are being taught by false teachers directly opposed to a biblical mindset, thought process, or belief system. If they do sense a problem, they will usually try to make the false belief system mesh with the Bible by taking Scripture out of context or by completely ignoring opposing Scripture—so they can follow the false belief system without any conviction from the Holy Spirit.

Here are some verses that deal with this issue and the subject of security in general:

> Until we all reach unity in the faith and in the knowledge
> of the Son of God and become mature, attaining to the
> whole measure of the fullness of Christ. Then we will
> no longer be infants, tossed back and forth by the waves,
> and blown here and there by every wind of teaching and
> by the cunning and craftiness of men in their deceitful
> scheming. Instead, speaking the truth in love, we will
> in all things grow up into him who is the Head, that is,
> Christ. (Ephesians 4:13-15)

I am challenged by this verse and will challenge you.

Do you want to stop being blown around by subjects, philosophies, professors, teachings or teachers, and the lies of Satan? Then read your Bible! Take faith-steps and see that God will not let you down. See that He is there. Grow in knowledge and understanding of Jesus Christ.

This means you will actually have to start studying your Bible. You might even want to go to some classes that your church offers instead of always just going to the worship service.

Memorize Scripture so it will be in your heart and mind throughout the day.

Here's a further challenge:

> If any of you lacks wisdom, he should ask God, who gives
> generously to all without finding fault, and it will be given
> to him. But when he asks, he must believe and not doubt,
> because he who doubts is like a wave of the sea, blown and
> tossed by the wind. That man should not think he will
> receive anything from the Lord; he is a double-minded
> man, unstable in all he does. (James 1:5-8)

This verse tells me to get rid of instability in my Christian life. I have to believe God. I need to ask and not doubt.

God will not always say what we want to hear. The wisdom from above will not always make us feel good. We will have to get rid of sin in our lives. We will have to sacrifice some things because our God is more important.

From this verse we learn that it is critical to kill doubt in any area of your Christian life! It is the thing that will most quickly hinder spiritual maturity. When doubt reigns, you don't realize that you are in its chains. You will not grow in understanding, because doubt will cloud over and choke out any understanding that might come along.

Doubt results in questions you might be unaware of. *Why do anything related to Christian service activities if you doubt that He cares what you do with your life? Why take any faith-step if you do not believe that God is even out there, much less that He is going to be there for you when you take a step out into the unknown?*

Doubt pleads with you to not believe in God and His power. It begs you to stay at your present maturity level because God is pleased with you and there is no reason for you to become a super-Christian; that is only for people in ministry positions. It fills your mind with objections and reasons not to believe the Bible because, after all, the Bible was written by King James, not God.

These are just a few of the absurdities that doubt throws in our faces.

Doubt, lack of biblical understanding, and lack of knowledge will either keep you from being secure in your faith and beliefs, or it will wither your security until you are back to being thrown around by every wind of teaching and doctrine that is not from God.

Be secure in your beliefs about God and His Word, and fight doubt whenever and wherever it comes.

SERVICE

This kind of service involves understanding that you are to be a faithful servant for the rest of your life. It is part of God's will and plan for your life to understand and live out the life of a servant. He is King, Lord, Savior, and God. Your life needs to reflect that this is true through your thoughts, feelings, and actions. If your life does not involve some semblance of servitude in all those areas, you will not be living out all of God's will and plan for you.

Here are some verses on service; the emphasis is mine.

"But be sure to fear the Lord and *serve* him faithfully with all your heart; consider what great things he has done for you" (1 Samuel 12:24).

"Whoever wants to become great among you must be your *servant*, and whoever wants to be first must be *slave* of all" (Mark 10:43-44).

"If I were still trying to please men, I would not be a *servant* of Christ" (Galatians 1:10).

"What does the Lord your God ask of you but to fear the Lord your God, to walk in all his ways, to love him, to *serve* the Lord your God with all your heart and with all your soul, and to observe the Lord's commands and decrees" (Deuteronomy 10:12-13).

"Live as free men, but do not use your freedom as a cover-up for evil; live as *servants* of God" (1 Peter 2:16).

"But if *serving* the Lord seems undesirable to you, then choose for yourselves this day whom you will *serve* . . . But as for me and my household, we will *serve* the Lord" (Joshua 24:15).

Take a minute and reread those verses. Let them speak to you. See the importance of service, of having a servant's heart, attitude, outlook, and life.

This part of God's will and plan for your life is under heavy attack now; it always has been. Since the beginning, God's people have had trouble with serving the Lord.

Why? Because we have a sinful nature bent on doing what *we* want to do instead of bending our knee and will to what *God* wants us to do. And whenever we are able to overcome our sinful nature, Satan is ready with his arsenal of lies, temptations, and anything else he can use to twist, destroy, and keep us from living out our lives as servants of God.

I envision this like a game that is played at amusement parks. It is the one that involves a person holding a hammer-like object (usually padded), and the object of the game is to try to hit things that pop up out of holes in a limited amount of time. I see Christians as the things that pop up out of the holes, and Satan is ready with a big hammer (that is *not* padded) to hit them when they come up. Christians only pop up when they are saved, ready to serve the Lord or recommit their lives. They are so happy, bubbly, and on-fire for God that they "pop" up and are going to live for God. Satan is waiting for this moment to hit them as hard as he can so he can stop them dead in their tracks.

Satan will use any way he can to kill your ambition for living for God. Maybe he fills your head full of lies: *Do you think God really wants to use someone like you? Could God really have called you into a life like this? You are not smart enough, trained enough, or knowledgeable enough to do that, so why don't you just give up? Did God really say _____? Don't go witness to your friends or take a stand for Jesus; you will stop being cool, and you might get made fun of, and you really don't want that, do you?*

He could also convince you to become so busy in church-related activities or service projects that you end up burning out and giving up. The old saying fits here: *If Satan can't make you lazy, he will make you busy!*

Then, when you go back down into the hole because you believed whatever Satan used, know that he is laughing at you. He is smiling down at you with an evil smile, saying, "Don't you ever get back up. You take a stand for God, Jesus, or anything that relates to truth, and I will be here to hit you again. I will bring an army of demons that you would not believe in order to keep you down there."

Sadly, most Christians go back down into the hole, never to resurface. They believe the lies, they give in to fear and doubt, and they never live their lives as servants of God.

You do not have to be part of that group. You can "pop" up and decide to live as a servant for God the rest of your life. You can rest in the knowledge that our God is bigger, stronger, and perfectly capable of dealing with anything Satan will try to hit you with. You can raise your shield of faith and extinguish any fiery dart the Devil throws at you. Use your shield to knock out some of Satan's teeth as he tries to devour you.

Will you be a servant of God? Will you have the right heart-attitude and be a slave to Christ? Or will you give in to Satan and serve him instead? If you are not serving God, you are either serving yourself or you are being a servant to Satan's lies, whims, and wants for your life.

There is no neutral ground.

SUFFERING

It is part of God's will and plan for every Christian to suffer and be persecuted because of the name of Jesus Christ. The type of persecution or suffering will vary in form and fashion for every Christian. The bottom line is that you will be made fun of, be physically harmed, lose your job, be run out of town, or be killed because of your Christian beliefs.

Christians in the United States do not understand this as easily as Christians in China, the Middle East, or other countries where belief in Jesus immediately means jail time or execution.

Here are some verses on suffering and persecution.

> Dear friends, do not be surprised at the painful trial you are suffering, as though something strange were happening to you. But rejoice that you participate in the sufferings of Christ, so that you may be overjoyed when his glory is revealed. If you are insulted because of the name of Christ, you are blessed, for the Spirit of glory and of God rests on you. If you suffer, it should not be as a murderer or thief or any other kind of criminal, or even as a meddler. However, if you suffer as a Christian, do not be ashamed, but praise God that you bear that name. For it is time for judgment to begin with the family of God; and if it begins with us, what will the outcome be for those who do not obey the gospel of God? And, "If it is hard for the righteous to be saved, what will become of the ungodly and the sinner?" So then, those who suffer according to God's will should commit themselves to their faithful Creator and continue to do good. (1 Peter 4:12-19)

These words from the book of John are from Jesus himself:

If the world hates you, keep in mind that it hated me first. If you belonged to the world, it would love you as its own. As it is, you do not belong to the world, but I have chosen you out of the world. That is why the world hates you. Remember the words I spoke to you: "No servant is greater than his master." If they persecuted me, they will persecute you also. If they obeyed my teaching, they will obey yours also. They will treat you this way because of my name, for they do not know the One who sent me. (John 15:18-21)

Not only so, but we also rejoice in our sufferings, because we know that suffering produces perseverance; perseverance, character; and character, hope. (Romans 5:3-4)

I consider that our present sufferings are not worth comparing with the glory that will be revealed in us. (Romans 8:18)

I recently read a quote by St. Augustine that fits here. "God had one son on earth without sin, but never one without suffering."

If the above quote is true, and the verses in 1 Peter are true, and the words of Jesus are true, then why do most Christians run around being dismayed as though something unbelievable is happening to them when they encounter suffering and persecution?

Since Jesus promised that the world would hate us and that we would be persecuted, why do preachers paint the Christian life-style as trouble-free and filled with happiness?

If we are supposed to rejoice in our suffering, why do we Christians go into a depression when we get made fun of, lose friends, lose a job, get physically hurt, or get arrested—all because we take a stand on our beliefs in the Bible or Jesus Christ?

It appears that all the answers have to deal with the lack of a biblical understanding, mindset, and worldview.

This was evident in a prayer meeting that my wife attended last year. She came home, and the first thing she said when she came in the door was, "Well, it's a good thing you weren't at that meeting." I knew this was going to be good.

While everyone was sharing prayer requests at the meeting, the parents of a college student who was going on a mission trip to India asked for special prayer. The mom shared, through tears, that the area her son was going to was so dangerous that some Christian missionaries to that area had been incarcerated or killed. Because of that, they would not know exactly where he was going or be able to contact him while he was over there.

She also shared how many members of the team, including her son, were having terrible nightmares of being tortured and killed. This even resulted in a few of them dropping out of the mission trip altogether. But her son was convinced that God wanted him to go on this mission trip, so he was resolved to go.

After the mother had shared this and asked for special prayer over her son, another mother decided to put in her own two-cents' worth. This was where my wife told me that if I had been there, I probably would have exploded into a ball of fire. I definitely would have been upset with what the other mother said.

She shared with the prayer group how ridiculous it was for Christians to even go to a dangerous place. She thought that Christians should go to places that are not at all dangerous for a mission trip, and even go to places where they could do some fun sightseeing while they were there. She finished her speech by informing everyone that Christians should not actually go to dangerous places like that, but if they wanted to, they should *just go and pray at the borders of dangerous countries.*

After I got over my initial firestorm reaction, I felt very sad. My heart and head hurt that a Christian woman who had been going to church for much of her life could think that way. I felt hurt for the parents of the son who was going to India, hurt that other Christians could ridicule their son and his probable sacrifice for the glory of God and the name of Jesus Christ.

I was dumbfounded by the fact that someone who sat in church, was at every prayer meeting, and seemingly read her Bible regularly could have such a gross misconception of what the Christian life really entails.

Should we expect to get made fun of for our beliefs? Yes!

Will we lose friends, hobbies, interests, and other aspects of our lives when we give control of our lives to God? Yes!

Will we offend people and suffer consequences for witnessing about Jesus? Yes!

Could God call you to go and die in some foreign country doing mission work? Yes!

Is the world going to hate us? Yes!

But will we to change the eternal destination for some of the people we witness to from hell to heaven? Yes!

Will we get rewards for suffering, being persecuted, getting made fun of, or dying for the gospel? *Yes!*

Our focus has to be on eternity and on the way God calls us to live. We cannot always be worrying about what other people think of us. Instead of valuing this worldly life and the things in it, we have to be resolved to go and do whatever God has for us. It does not matter what end is in store for us.

Know that it is God's will and plan for your life to go through some suffering and persecution.

If you never go through any of that, I will be bold enough to say that you are staying in your comfort zone and living a limited and possibly fake Christian life.

You are deliberately rejecting God's voice or the impression of the Holy Spirit when He comes and challenges you to witness to unbelievers. When God pushes you to go on a mission trip, you run away because you might actually have to sacrifice money, time, or your life in following God—and those things are just more important than God is.

When you live like that, you need to be honest with yourself and take a long look in the mirror. Realize that if you never follow God into any kind of faith-step, never witness to anyone because of whatever fear you feel, or just think that Christians should never suffer or be persecuted because God is all about love and wouldn't let that happen to anyone, *then you have believed and are happily living out a lie from Satan.*

You are living a lukewarm Christian life at best, with no sacrifice or risk on the horizon.

Is it any wonder that Jesus went around saying repeatedly, "O ye of little faith"?

SPECIFIC ASPECTS THAT ARE GOD'S WILL FOR YOU

SURRENDER

This aspect reminds me of watching cartoons while growing up. In the cartoons, there would be fights, usually between a good guy and a bad guy. These characters took turns tricking each other and blowing one another up. The battle ended with the bad guy in a crumpled heap, sticking an arm out of the mess and waving a white flag. He was surrendering because he'd had enough.

I like that symbolism in regards to how we need to approach surrendering to God's will for our lives. After fighting God, going down our own avenues of what we want to do—even deliberately running away from what God wants us to do—if we are eventually serious about our relationship with God, we will surrender.

We will put aside everything and humbly lay down our lives at God's feet. We will stop fighting; we will stop running; and we will give up control. We will say, "Okay, God, I am now your prisoner. You are my King and Lord. I will do whatever you want me to do." We need to have this kind of heart-attitude for the long journey of the Christian life that is ahead of us. Luke 14:26-33 says:

> If anyone comes to me and does not hate his father and mother, his wife and children, his brothers and sisters— yes, even his own life—he cannot be my disciple. And anyone who does not carry his cross and follow me cannot be my disciple. Suppose one of you wants to build a tower. Will he not first sit down and estimate the cost to see if he has enough money to complete it? For if he lays the foundation and is not able to finish it, everyone who sees it will ridicule him, saying, "This fellow began to build and was not able to finish."

Or suppose a king is about to go to war against another king. Will he not first sit down and consider whether he is able with ten thousand men to oppose the one coming against him with twenty thousand? If he is not able, he will send a delegation while the other is still a long way off and will ask for terms of peace. In the same way, any of you who does not give up everything he has cannot be my disciple."

This passage encapsulates much of what surrendering entails. Our love for our family and our own lives needs to look like hate compared to the love we have for Jesus. We surrender the right to love anyone or anything else more than Christ.

Our lives need to reflect the fact that we carry our cross and follow Jesus. We surrender the right or desire to follow anyone or anything else.

Our choices are controlled by "counting the cost." We surrender the right to give up halfway through something we know God has called us to do. In doing this, we will not be ridiculed, be looked upon as someone who does not keep his word, or reflect poorly on Christ.

We also surrender the right to plan something we cannot finish or to plan something inadequately.

Jesus says to "give up everything." So why do we read that and then spend our lives holding on tightly? When we surrender to God, we do not hold on to anything. This includes our dreams or aspirations for our lives, our thoughts on how life is supposed to be, and our habits, hobbies, and leisure activities.

Do not hold on to anything that takes precedence over your complete dedication and willing obedience to Jesus Christ and the Word of God! Be prepared for your Lord and King to take things away, even if they are not a problem in your life.

Am I saying that we are not supposed to have any fun in life or do things we enjoy? Of course not! I am saying that everything is up for grabs when we surrender to Jesus. He gets to decide what leisure activities we get to do, and if anything comes between us or starts to become more important than spending time with Him, then we need to surrender it.

COMMITMENT

In your life you will need to commit to fulfilling God's specific plan and will. When God calls you to do something in your life, no matter how big or small, He wants you to stay committed.

As Christians, we do not give up when life gets tough. We do not chicken out when it gets scary or when we think it's too overwhelming. When God sets out His plan and will for our life, we stay the course, whatever the course may be. We run the race, we persevere when the race is grueling, and then we finish the race.

Hebrews 12:1b–2a says, "Let us throw off everything that hinders and the sin that so easily entangles, and let us run with perseverance the race marked out for us. Let us fix our eyes on Jesus, the author and perfecter of our faith."

We should want to say, as Paul did in 2 Timothy 4:7, "I have fought the good fight, I have finished the race, I have kept the faith." This was Paul's perspective at the end of his life.

We can say this as well when we do God's will and live out God's plan for our lives. We cannot say this when we ignore God and what He wants us to do. We cannot say it if we give up halfway through. We cannot say it if we are cowards and never overcome whatever fears keep us from running or finishing the race. We cannot say it if we never start running.

A few years ago, we had the pleasure of having a missionary couple over for dinner. Nothing could have prepared me for how much their visit would reshape my thinking about commitment. They had been on the mission field for twenty-five years. After sharing with us where they had been in Africa, our kids quizzed them on what kinds of animals they had seen, and we shared with them that we were missionaries as well. My wife and I said we were amazed at how hard missionary work is. We told them how thankful we were to have missionaries like them in our house and said that they inspired us to keep going. They sat back, smiled, and then proceeded to shock my idea of faith and commitment to its very core.

The wife leaned forward and said, "Do you know that, for twenty-three of the twenty-five years, we saw no fruit from our labors?"

She smiled fondly as she explained. "After the first couple of years, my husband and I began questioning our calling from God. We wondered why He would send us to a place where no one was listening or showing the slightest interest in the Bible. My husband began to wonder if we were in the wrong place, since there were no conversions and nobody wanted to have anything to do with Christianity or the Bible.

"After praying and praying, God finally answered our prayers, but not in the way we imagined. My husband felt God ask him, *Am I not worth it? Is the work you do worthless if no one ever comes to a worship meeting or a Bible study?* He admitted through tears that the work was still worth our lives, even if nothing ever happened.

"For twenty-three years we saw nothing happen, and then a flood of fruit came. Some of the men that had been coming to worship meetings and Bible studies for years began to give their lives to Christ. My husband had so much work to do, he didn't know what to do with himself. Several families got saved, and some of the men even surrendered to the call of being involved in ministry. So my husband began to spend more and more time training the men to be preachers and leaders. There were several men that ended up leaving their villages to go to the missionary Bible college that was far away. This education was very time-consuming and created a burden for their families while they were away. But they returned as strong men of God and leaders in their villages and communities.

"We had to leave when we were forced to retire. It was heartbreaking for us to leave while all the excitement was going on, just when it seemed that God was accomplishing a powerful work among the people. Someone else came and carried on our work, and we hear from the people we stay in contact with that there is still much going on."

She finished her memories with something that has gnawed at me ever since: "I now know that God had been working through all the first twenty-three years. We were faithful to keep tilling the soil—even while we worried, doubted, and felt useless, since we saw no results. I wonder what would have happened if we had just given up. I'm sure that God would have provided us with a different job. But what would have happened to those villages and those men? I don't know and can't say for sure, but I think nothing would have happened. God is faithful, no matter how long it takes. Why can't we be more faithful and committed to Him?"

I still marvel at the level of commitment of that missionary couple. It would be nice to think that I could have that level of commitment in my life in doing what God wanted me to do. However, when I look back at my record of remaining committed during hard times, times of doubt, and times when I could not see God working, I realize that my faith was not as strong as theirs. I would have chalked it up to the idea that God must have been closing the door to that missionary work, and I would have left Africa long before twenty-three years had come and gone.

All my expectations and supposed hearing of God's will and plan for my life would have been based on results. The absence of results or fruits from our labors would have equaled a fast, one-way ticket out of there. Surely God would not want us to continue working someplace where our skills and gifts could not be seen to produce anything. I mean, I don't have a master's degree from a seminary for nothing. I would have assumed that God had a different place for us, a place where we could *really* be doing His work and seeing His accomplishments.

Although this would have been my own reaction, this kind of thinking is completely wrong and very unbiblical. In Scripture we see men and women who were committed like the missionary couple was. We see people who followed God when it did not make any sense at all. And to add insult to the confusion of an unclear or nonsensical path, they were made fun of while following God.

Take Noah and Joshua, for example.

Noah built a boat and preached salvation for those who would get on the boat before the flood came. In return, he got no converts, and I can imagine all the heckling and clever insults that were thrown at him by his neighbors.

God told Joshua to march around Jericho several times, blowing trumpets and yelling and then the walls would fall down, and he and his men would be able to go in. Can you imagine the strange looks he got when he explained the plan to his commanders? I imagine he knew that some of them thought he had lost his mind and were just waiting for this plan to fail so they could laugh and mock him—or even try to replace him as leader of Israel.

But what happened in the end? Things worked out just as God said they would.

Sadly, those who don't heed God's call are in peril of suffering. Many people would have survived if they had listened to Noah and come aboard the ark. Many people would not be in hell for eternity if they had just listened to the gospel, if they had just believed in God's Son.

You fail to listen to God's plan and will for your life at your own peril. I believe that you will not achieve or accomplish what God has for you to do on this earth if you do not follow and stay committed to His plan and will for your life. You will not get to hear "Well done, good and faithful servant" when you die. You will have few or no rewards in heaven, no crowns to throw at our Savior's feet. Follow God and stay committed to Him—even when you see no fruit, when it doesn't make sense, and when it is hard.

There are some of you reading this who still have no clue about what God's will or plan is for your life. Nearly every time I have the privilege of speaking or teaching on this topic, I am cornered afterward and asked, "Can you tell me how I can know what God's will is for my life? Or let me tell you a little about myself, and then you can probably tell me what God wants me to do."

I have an amazing answer for these people. Are you ready for it? Are you ready to have all your questions answered about God's will and plan for your life?

I have no clue about what specific job or task God wants you to do in this life. We have already discussed basic, general aspects of God's will and plan for your life. We have even talked about two specific aspects that God wants in your heart-attitude as you follow His will for your life.

But the question is this: how can you find out what God's will and plan is for your life specifically? Know now that there are preachers, authors, and other authorities who will tell you that they know *exactly* how to answer that question. If *I* knew the answer to that question, I could write a book or sell the formula in church and make millions.

The answer is that *only God knows.* You are going to have to seek out God and listen to Him, if you plan on finding out what His will and plan really are for your life. Even though I said there is no magic formula for knowing God's will, I will give you some direction. (Here I am guilty of one of my own pet peeves. Preachers or authors say that nobody on earth can know something, but they think *they* know, even though they really don't. And then they proceed to tell you what they think. Anyway, enough of my pet peeves.)

What can you do to maximize your ability to hear God clearly?

- Read your Bible daily.
- Pray to God daily, or even better, pray without ceasing.
- Have a quiet time with God daily.
- Memorize Scripture.

It boils down to having daily contact with God. It is as easy at that. Are you going to be serious about your relationship with God?

This next checklist is by no means exhaustive or the final word on knowing God's will and plan for your life.

How can I be sure what God's will is for my life?

- *There is confirmation in God's Word.*

As you read His Word and meditate on Scripture, there will be no doubt when God is confirming His will in your life. It will be up to you to have faith, believe, and then take faith-steps to follow it.

- *Advice from godly counselors and other Christians will line up with what God has impressed upon your heart, mind, or soul.*

It will be as if you hear God's voice through them. They will confirm things that God has already impressed upon you, or you will recognize through the Holy Spirit that they are speaking words of truth to you. Again, it will be up to you to listen, believe, and follow.

This guideline can be a little tricky, as I learned before going to the mission field. If you already know the will of God for your life, please do not go to a godly counselor or mentor and get confused by whatever happens afterward.

This happened when I was filled with excitement to tell one of the most influential Christian mentors in my life about the next step God was calling me to take in my life. He was an old cowboy preacher who did campus ministry very well. As we were driving home from the mission trip that changed my life, I remember talking to him about going to seminary. I told him that I felt God revealing in my heart that I would have to go to seminary in order to get a Christian counseling degree. Then I complained that I would never have the financial means to afford seminary. I remember him slowing down the vehicle to look me straight in the eyes and assure me with firmness that if God wanted me to go to seminary He would provide the financial means to accomplish that.

To make a long story short, God provided tuition for every semester we were at the seminary. It was an awesome, faith-building time. I remember hanging on His words while we were there. When it didn't look like bills were going to get paid, or tuition was going to be a major concern, God always provided. Sometimes it was through individuals, other times through churches. All in all, my mentor's words, which struck me to the heart, rang true and were easily backed up by Scripture.

Now, fast-forward to a time after seminary—after quitting my counseling job and after waiting six or seven months for God to reveal the job that He would have me do.

I was driving with my wife, full of excitement, to tell this great spiritual mentor in my life about what God had called us to do. I was nervous and happy. I couldn't wait to tell him that it was campus ministry, and because of his history with campus ministry jobs, I just knew he would be ecstatic. I greatly anticipated any wise words he might say that I could hold on to while on the mission field. Before getting out of the car, my wife reached over and squeezed my hand, smiling and telling me she hadn't seen me that excited in a while.

Jumping out of the car, I went to knock on my friend's door, but he was already coming out because he had to go somewhere. So I excitedly told him that my wife and I knew beyond a shadow of a doubt that God had called us to move to Colorado and do campus ministry work. I told him that we would have to raise all of our funds to go out there and do missionary work.

As I looked at him and waited for a response, I almost couldn't contain myself in waiting for him to be happy with me and to speak wisdom into my life.

Much to my dismay, he glared at me and responded in an angry tone. He asked me if I knew how crazy all this sounded. He told me to think about what this was going to do to my young family, since I was going to be moving them so far away from home, family, and friends. He continued to berate me for my lack of knowledge in how hard missionary life was. He closed with how his church could not help fund our ministry because they were too overburdened.

I remember mumbling my good-byes and turning to walk away. He glanced at me disapprovingly one more time and then hurriedly climbed into his pickup truck and left. I climbed back into the car with my wife and sat there, dumbfounded. She asked me what had happened, because from where she sat it didn't look like it had gone very well. I could not even respond. I sat with silent tears running down my cheeks, because I was so hurt.

This whole episode confused me, until God answered my questioning prayers about a week or two later. All He said was, "Are you going to listen to men, or are you going to listen to Me?"

I conceded that I would listen to Him.

That experience has helped enormously in following God's will and plan for my life. I understand now that it was His way of breaking me from following men's voices and looking to different preachers, mentors, or Christians I respected to be God's voice in my life. It makes it easier when you just listen to God's impressions in your life, instead of running around to five different people to see if their advice matches up with what God has told you to do.

I hope the subtle difference here is clear. Godly counselors, mentors, and advisors can and will line up with what God's will is for your life. They can even be the voice that God speaks through in order to encourage, motivate, and strengthen you to follow God's will and plan for your life.

But *do not* run to them when God has already revealed what to do in your life, or you might have to be broken from listening to men's voices. Again, I am dealing specifically with the topic of God's will. I don't want you to think that I never look to godly advisors or mentors for advice or help. Just last week I went to a godly man for advice on how to manage my time better, because I was having serious problems in that area. It helped immensely.

- *God's peace is present.*

I have learned to rely on this one as a confirming factor in knowing God's will for my life. It happened in making the decision to go to seminary, and I didn't even know what it was. I remember walking around at the seminary with my wife, and she kept asking me if I felt God speaking or leading us to go there. I told her I really didn't feel anything at that moment except a sense of peace if we chose to go there.

It was more of a mind-numbing, complete-body peace that overcame me when I went in to quit my counseling job with no job in sight for the future. I couldn't even explain how calm and peaceful I was—in what should have been a not-so-peace-filled moment.

When we traveled to Colorado to tour campuses, I remember praying for God to reveal His will at the campus where we are serving now. He answered later that it was going to be a war. There would be much spiritual warfare, lots of hard work, and rough times ahead if we were going to work there. After praying with my wife and driving around the town some more, we felt the peace of God. It doesn't make much sense that we would feel peaceful while surrendering to go to a war zone. But it makes perfect sense if you look through biblical glasses.

If we follow God's will and plan for our life even when it doesn't make sense—even when it hurts emotionally, financially, or physically or when it is rough and tough—we will experience the peace of God somewhere amidst all of that. If we base our thinking, feelings, and actions on the Word of God, we will have peace, even while the war or storm rages around us.

Jesus gave us His words about peace. In the book of John, He spoke to His disciples shortly before His crucifixion—words that ring true to us today.

"I have told you these things, so that in me you may have peace. In this world you will have trouble. But take heart! I have overcome the world" (John 16:33).

We need to have peace and shine an example of peace-filled living, even in the middle of troubling times, so that unbelievers and believers alike will see that this is how Christians live.

Paul gave us great words to calm our souls as well: "The Lord is near. Do not be anxious about anything, but in everything, by prayer and petition, with thanksgiving, present your requests to God. And the peace of God, which transcends all understanding, will guard your hearts and your minds in Christ Jesus" (Philippians 4:5b-7).

Let me share some closing remarks about God's will and plan for your life.

- Remember to be patient and to wait on God.
- Be ruthlessly honest with yourself in seeking, surrendering, and following God's will in your life.
- Use your brain. God created us with the ability to think. *He guides our minds as we think things through in His presence and through His Word.*
- Don't listen to the world and its desires!
- Don't listen to your flesh and its desires!
- Remember that unbelievers and believers alike may try to lead you astray from God's will and plan for your life.

If we can just get the foundation of our Christian belief system built right, we will never be led astray. Some good, bottom-layer building blocks would be these: God is in control, and He has a plan for your life.

The trouble is that most "fake" Christians build their beliefs on the world, on lies from Satan, and on beliefs that come from loving, living by, and giving in to their sinful nature.

Don't give in, don't give up, and definitely don't quit. God is in control. He cares for you, He will guide you through anything, and He is always there for you. If you feel like you can't get through, wait on Him—or investigate whether some of your sin is causing problems for you.

God has a plan for your life. It will be a fantastic journey if you follow Him in faith-steps and in His Word. I wish we could sit down over a cup of coffee years from now and tell each other what has happened in our lives as we both followed God's will for us. Start living and doing it now! Otherwise, you will just have to listen to *me* talk years from now, and it would be a sad commentary on your Christian life if you had nothing to share.

Remember, at the end of this life, it will not be God's fault if we have not lived for Him. It will be ours.

CHAPTER 3

Thinking

We demolish arguments and every pretension that sets
itself up against the knowledge of God, and we take
captive every thought to make it obedient to Christ.
—2 Corinthians 10:5

If Christians in general would let this be one of the foundational
verses on how to think in this life, it would change the face of
Christianity across this world. Take some time to meditate on the
above verse. Commit it to memory. Has it already expanded or
refined the way you think? Does it convict you about thought
processes that are not consistent with what this verse calls us to do
as Christians?

A lesson I taught on this verse caused us the most trouble and drama
to date as campus ministers. I remember being excited about teaching
the lesson. In my short experience as a Christian speaker, I have noticed
that some lessons and sermons burn brighter in my heart and mind than
others do. It's like I am bottled up and just can't wait to pour out what
God has filled me with. Even if I don't see results from the lesson or
sermon, I am still happy and feel that God is using me mightily as the
Holy Spirit speaks through me. On this particular occasion, I knew that
this was going to be one of those times.

The night usually goes like this: we eat a meal together, sing a few worship songs, and end with a video, sermon, or interactive lesson with discussion at the end.

When it was time for the lesson, I looked around and was very encouraged by the fact that we had the most students we had ever had at one of our meetings. This was easy to tell, since we usually averaged around fifteen students, and that night we had approximately thirty students.

As I was speaking, I could tell that the lesson was encouraging some students while offensively slapping others in the face. A lot of them nodded their heads and smiled agreement. Others looked at me as if I was a raving lunatic.

The main focus of my words made it clear that *demolishing arguments* and *taking every thought captive* was not exactly positive or easy imagery. As college students especially, they needed to take seriously the battleground of the mind and all the false beliefs that are perpetuated on the college campus. Finally, I challenged them to identify some arguments and pretensions that needed to be destroyed in their lives or on their campus, and to pinpoint thoughts they needed to imprison and make obedient to Christ.

When I opened it up for discussion, the firestorm started. I found out why one group's demeanor showed disagreement when they informed me that they were all atheists except for one Buddhist. They explained to me how my kind of talk was exactly what they hated about Christianity.

They accosted me with rhetorical questions and ultimatums: How were people ever supposed to learn and grow if all they believed was the Bible? Didn't I know that Jesus was just a fictional figure that had never really walked the earth—or a historical person who was just a good teacher and not the Son of God? Where was the freedom to decide between right and wrong if you made every thought captive to Christ? Surely I did not believe that every other religion on the face of the earth was wrong except for Christianity, did I?

They went on to say that they had heard that we had a good group that was very loving and fun—but, boy, had they heard wrong. This went on for a little while, until the Buddhist looked at me with a very arrogant, almost demonic look on her face and asked, "Well, what do you believe happens to someone who dies without believing in Jesus Christ?" I did what any good, cowardly campus minister would do; I opened it up for others to respond to the question before I did.

It actually went a whole lot better than I ever envisioned it would. Three strong Christian students explained why they believed what they believed, what the Word of God had to say on that subject, and shared their testimonies.

The Buddhist accepted their stories with no offense and then shared everything that she believed in her belief system. She explained at length about the different chakras, how she aspired to get a purple halo, and her beliefs on the afterlife. At the end of her talk, she added that she had grown up in a Christian home but left the faith because all of the "fake" people that went to church. She told us how other religions were not as limiting as the Christian faith system, how Buddhism had opened her mind to new heights she'd never thought she could attain, and how she was at peace with the world through Buddhism. She reiterated that the Bible was the most ridiculous book that she had ever read and that it was full of contradictions. She scoffed at our belief in Jesus and said that she firmly believed that he was a made-up character that had never truly walked the earth.

This resulted in some of the Christian students objecting to that last statement and informing her that many secular historians verified that Jesus Christ was a real man. These students encouraged her to take a look at the ample evidence on that subject. I had to intervene, because it was about to get ugly.

I asked her and the other atheists if they would like to hear what I believed the Christian answer was to her earlier question. (I should have known that this would sound offensive to her, but sometimes I am not too bright.) I explained in a loving way that if we take Scripture in a literal sense, as it was written, that it is very easy to answer the question about what happens to people who do not believe in Jesus Christ or the Bible. I quickly went through Romans' "road of salvation"[2] and stressed the importance of how sin separates us from God. Only belief

---

[2]   Romans 3:23, Romans 6:23, Romans 5:8, and Romans 10:9-10.

in Jesus Christ and his resurrection bridges the gap that we can never bridge ourselves. If a person does not believe this, he will spend eternity separated from the God that loves him—in hell.

That is where the meeting pretty much broke down. She could not believe that a Christian nowadays would hold to such antiquated beliefs. Was I not aware that most Christians did not even believe in hell anymore?

In retrospect, I should have been trying to end the discussion long before this point, but again I am not too bright. So I tried to stop the discussion on that topic, offered to talk with her afterward on the subject, and then opened the evening up to any other thoughts or comments. This was where it went from bad to much, much worse.

A girl who had not attended the meeting in a while was there that night, and she talked about how she had noticed that there were many Mormons in the community and at the college. She went on to express her dismay at how they believed in the book of Mormon when there was no historical or archaeological evidence to support it—but that there was abundant evidence for the Bible. This took the discussion in a very bad direction because, in her absence, committed Mormons had been coming to the group. I had always tiptoed around Mormonism, because I wanted to build a relationship with them before hitting them with the truth. She did not know that they had come every week for a long time. Furthermore, on this night they had spent a long time preparing the desserts for our meeting. (They were these awesomely delicious root beer float cupcakes. I had never heard of such things and, boy, were they good!) Needless to say, this was the worst time the girl could have said what she did, even if it was true.

It all went downhill after that. One Mormon girl interrupted her and yelled about how that wasn't right or true. Then she and her friends left in tears. The Buddhist and the other atheists raged about the carelessness of Christians and how intolerant they were of other religions. One Christian male student did a great job of defusing the situation by explaining how we should talk to each other in love and never handle the situation the way it had just been handled. He reminded the atheists and the Buddhist that not one of the Christians in the room had taken offense to their truly derogatory and offensive remarks about the Bible and our Savior Jesus Christ. He pointed out that the girl had never gotten to finish sharing her beliefs once she'd started. He also begged them to give the same consideration and respect to Christian beliefs that had been given to their explanations and beliefs. They sullenly agreed that he was right.

I stopped the discussion after that and quickly ended it with a word of prayer. Several Christian students came up afterward with varying opinions on how the night had gone. Some were very encouraged and challenged. Others were upset that the discussion had gotten out of hand. The Christian girl who had invited all the atheists and the Buddhist was very excited that they had gotten to hear the plan of salvation and to explain their beliefs with no one ridiculing them for it.

As I was leaving, the Buddhist came back and caught me in the hallway. She had anger written all over her face and tears in her eyes and wanted to inform me of how horrible a job I'd done. She thought I should have moderated the discussion better and said how insensitive we Christians are as a whole. She was insulted and felt that her faith had been attacked. She went on to tell me how dumb I was in believing what I believed and that she would never come back to our meeting. I apologized for the way the discussion had gone, and I agreed with her that it definitely could have gone better. I informed her that it was our third semester on the campus, and I was still very new to campus ministry. I ended with another apology, and she stormed off, muttering how bad we were as leaders and that the Christian students in attendance were awful, horribly inconsiderate idiots.

As my wife and I drove home, we were happy and upset at the same time. We were really happy to have had so many students attending and pleased that the unbelievers had heard the gospel presented in so many different ways. We were sad about what had happened to the Mormon girls and that some of the unbelievers had been so angry and upset during the arguing. We decided that we needed rules for discussions and would implement them in the meetings to come. Little did we know that all of this would almost get us kicked off the campus.

The Buddhist and Mormon went to the head of campus ministry and some administrators of the college, informing them of everything that had happened—from their points of view. Over the next week, I spent most of my time explaining exactly what had happened to several people. I was amazed at how often I was threatened about getting kicked off campus, and that people were looking into taking legal action against our ministry.

I again took time to explain exactly what had happened and who had really insulted whom. I asked these people if we had lost the freedom of speech that we as Americans were supposed to have. When I asked them if it was healthy for everyone to be able to express what they truly believed at a meeting like that, they agreed wholeheartedly that it was. When I asked if it was healthy to discuss varying beliefs, they said yes. They even agreed that things would probably get heated and needed to be handled in a healthy manner. I informed them that I thought I'd done a horrible job keeping control of the discussion and that I learned a great deal from that night. Even with all this agreement, the time ended in a strange and pretty unfair manner.

They concluded that all this was good, but they reminded me that I could not speak in such ways on a college campus. If I was working out of the united campus ministry office, I could never tell anyone that they were wrong—even though I hadn't. They agreed with the freedom of speech, but they informed me that students could never talk to each other that way.

I asked them if they ever had disagreements in science, politics, and other subjects. They answered that they did and that those discussions and disagreements were healthy and that students learned a great deal from them. When I told them I thought that was what was happening in our group, they emphatically told me I was wrong. Religion was different. They reminded me how intolerant it was to tell anyone what to believe or to say that they were wrong. They ended the meeting with veiled threats that if anything like this ever happened again, we would no longer be able to meet on campus.

I shared this remembrance to illustrate how the battle of ideas, thinking, and believing what you believe is raging. Satan has a stronghold on most universities and the world in general. When you bring the truth to a secular university—or even to most Christian ones today—expect a fight to the death. It will not be a fair fight either.

People will say they believe in freedom of speech; it just doesn't include the freedom to speak about Christian ideas or beliefs. They will tell you that everyone has a right to believe, follow, and practice their beliefs—unless you believe that everyone else is wrong. You cannot think like that; you have to believe that everyone is right in whatever they believe. These people will inform you that it is a grievous crime and inhuman error to ever tell someone what to believe or how to think. This is the moral relativism that has infected the majority of thinking in our country and within Christianity in general. It is completely wrong, biased, and unfair. Just be prepared for this to continue and get worse.

UNHEALTHY THINKING

When Christians have their minds filled with unhealthy thoughts, it will kill the Holy Spirit's ability to work in their lives. God expects us to renew our minds as we grow through sanctification and mature as Christians. Any thought contrary to the Word of God or the Holy Spirit's leading in our lives is in the realm of unhealthy thinking.

The majority of Christians do a great job at filling their minds with unhealthy thinking. It's like we have earplugs in our ears and then our hands firmly covering our ears, all in order to keep the Holy Spirit, God, or the Word of God from being able to penetrate our thinking. Instead of depending on the Bible to frame our thinking, we gladly follow any line of thinking that pleases us. If there is a sin listed in the Bible that we struggle with, our minds are at work trying to figure out some reason to justify being engaged in that sin. We will excuse it away with whatever reason, justification, or line of logic we can come up with to make ourselves feel better. It is usually very silly and appalling to us when we take a step back and think objectively about how we were lead astray by sinful, unhealthy thinking.

Some Christians will allow themselves to view pornography, for whatever reason, and will be convinced that there is no sin involved in it. But when they are confronted with the words of Jesus in Matthew 5:28, "But I tell you that anyone who looks at a woman lustfully has already committed adultery with her in his heart," how do they respond?

I hope it is evident to both men and women that if we look at the opposite sex lustfully we have already sinned in our hearts. So it is important to never justify a sin or sinful thought process and think that we are okay. Strangely enough, there are Christians who will read the above sentences in this paragraph and will still follow sinful, unhealthy thinking to give themselves an excuse to continue to be involved in pornography. I use pornography to make this point, but this line of thinking can be used to excuse *any* kind of sin that Christians want to be trapped in.

God is not silent on how important our thinking is, so why do most of us Christians live as if He is? Is it because we know that if we surrender our minds and thoughts to the process of renewal and transformation by God, everything will change? Is our need for control or our desire to stay in sin so strong that we will not heed His call to change our thinking?

I would beg you to start changing your thinking today. Pray that God will show you where your thinking is sinful and offensive to Him. Pray that He will reveal where your thinking has caused you to get off the straight and narrow path that you should be on.

Don't fight against it when God reveals sinful or anti-biblical ways of thinking—even those you may have held the majority of your life or learned at church.

HEALTHY THINKING

We can depend on God's word to strengthen, convict, refine, and show us the error in our thinking. The result is more godly and Christ-like thinking and thoughts. The next verses give insight on how negative thinking and sinful living result in some pretty stiff words from God. As you read them, let God work on your mind and show you what He would want for you to learn. The end result will be you taking a step in the direction of healthy thinking.

"In his pride the wicked does not seek him; in all his thoughts there is no room for God" (Psalm 10:4).

"The Lord detests the thoughts of the wicked, but those of the pure are pleasing to him" (Proverbs 15:26).

"For although they knew God, they neither glorified him as God nor gave thanks to him, but their thinking became futile and their foolish hearts were darkened" (Romans 1:21).

"Those who live according to the sinful nature have their minds set on what that nature desires" (Romans 8:5).

"Many live as enemies of the cross of Christ. Their destiny is destruction, their god is their stomach, and their glory is their shame. Their mind is on earthly things" (Philippians 3:18b–19).

These verses tell me several things about our thoughts:

- When our thoughts are consumed with pride and arrogance, there is no room for God or the Holy Spirit.
- God hates the thoughts of wicked people.
- God is pleased at pure thoughts.
- Even when we know God, it is a short step to letting our thinking become useless, which results in sinful darkness taking over our Christian lives.
- When we live according to our own sinful nature, we don't even realize that our minds are controlled by the desires of sin. We are consumed with directly opposing God and whatever is truly good, righteous, and holy. I hope we all do not want to be in direct opposition to how we are supposed to be living, thinking, and growing to become more Christlike.
- We are enemies of our salvation when we let our minds be controlled by sin and earthly desires, pursuits, and passions.

- The things that are glorified in this world—things like money, sex, status, living for oneself, and hedonistic lifestyles—are to be associated with shame. On judgment day, these trivial sin pursuits will take on a whole different level of shame— especially when individuals stand before God and realize that the things they gloried in on this earth were complete and utter acts of sin in the face of the holy, living God. We will be confronted by the truth and see clearly these lies given to us by Satan and our sinful nature.

Christians need to step up to the task of renewing and committing their minds to God. Destroy sinful thinking. Take captive every thought and make it obedient to Christ. We need to be able to truthfully say as Paul did in 1 Corinthians 2:16b, "But we have the mind of Christ."

Our minds and thoughts have to be set apart from this world and its sinful way of thinking. Part of "having the mind of Christ" involves overcoming anything that prevents us from doing the will of God in our lives. This means not feeding our minds and thoughts with lies from Satan and sinful thinking. Authentic and genuine Christians do not happily follow sin-filled thoughts that result in a life full of sinful actions.

This only scratches the surface of how important our thinking is to God. Get into reading your Bible, and find out how God feels about our thoughts. It's all in there, from beginning to end.

CHAPTER 4

Feelings and Emotions

But when the cross is working deeply, a believer comes
to know himself. He realizes how undependable are his
ideas, feelings, and desires.
—Watchman Nee

We live in a world consumed with feelings and emotions. For some, feelings decide how their day is going to be. Others let emotions influence what they think about a great many things. Feelings of hate drive human beings to do unspeakable acts to each other and themselves. Feelings of love may shape a young girl's thinking, and so she starts planning out her wedding from the age of seven. So, how is the Christian supposed to approach feelings and emotions? Are they good? Are they bad? When can you trust them? When are they not trustworthy? These are important questions to consider.

Let's define what we are talking about. I like one definition of *emotion* that is from an old sermon for which—for the life of me—I cannot find the citation. This sermon defined an emotion as "a strong feeling, a disturbance, a departure from the normal, calm state of rational thinking and acting. An impulse toward an action that has not been reasoned and approved by the mind."

Moods are closely associated with our emotions. A mood is basically a *predominant emotion.* It's an emotion that lasts a long time and leads to a change in behavior because of it.

No matter what age we are, emotions and feelings affect us dramatically. There are times in our lives when some of the feelings and emotions burn brighter than others. This is true throughout life stages as well. During adolescence, sexual feelings or emotions associated with love can be the ones that dominate the mind and body. During the golden years of life, depression and hopelessness may be trying to control feelings. Needless to say, emotions and feelings are a very big part of our lives while here on earth.

So what are we as Christians supposed to do with our emotions and feelings? I propose that we need to be striving for emotional stability. This may sound like psycho-babble, but I think it is very biblical. Galatians 5:19-26 says:

> The acts of the sinful nature are obvious; sexual immorality, impurity and debauchery; idolatry and witchcraft; hatred, discord, jealousy, fits of rage, selfish ambition, dissensions, factions and envy; drunkenness, orgies, and the like. I warn you, as I did before, that those who live like this will not inherit the kingdom of God.
>
> But the fruit of the Spirit is love, joy, peace, patience, kindness, goodness, faithfulness, gentleness and self-control. Against such things there is no law. Those who belong to Christ Jesus have crucified the sinful nature with its passions and desires. Since we live by the Spirit, let us keep in step with the Spirit. Let us not become conceited, provoking and envying each other.

This Scripture and much of the Bible paint a picture of feelings, thoughts, and actions intertwined. There are consequences for letting your emotions get the best of you and affect your thinking and actions—just as there are rewards for maturing and getting a handle on the reins of your emotions, so to speak.

Let's talk about emotional stability for a little while.

The first step in the direction of emotional stability is emotional maturity. Emotional maturity for the Christian involves letting the fruit of the Spirit dominate one's feelings and emotions. When we operate on these emotions, thoughts, and actions, our witness to the unbelieving world and Christian community will be undeniable.

We will also find freedom and peace in our own emotional realm. Since we will not be controlled by the flesh and the obvious sins that result from that, we will not feel guilty and full of shame because of the acts of the flesh. Will there still be struggles against the flesh and sin? Of course. But it will not be a constant battle that takes up all of our time and physical, mental, and emotional energy.

With the fruit of the Spirit as our goal for emotional control, there are some obvious results. We will care more about loving God and about God's love for us than we do about anything we love—or the world wants us to love—in this world. A commitment to being faithful in whatever God wants in our lives will overcome sinful, fleshly acts that we may have been engaged in for a long time. Maybe you have had a problem with fits of rage or hatred; maybe your family has taught you by example, or maybe you yourself have let this become a problem that you now cannot control. When we let gentleness and self-control flow from us, it will be hard for fits of rage and hatred to grab control of our feelings and actions.

The second aspect of emotional maturity involves growing from a state of self-centeredness to a state of outgoing concern for others. This is easily seen in infants and children. We have to teach them to share, to understand that everything is not mine, mine, mine!

This is true for emotionally immature Christians as well. We have to learn that this world and our Christian lives do not exist for me, me, me! It makes witnessing so much easier when we are more concerned about the soul of another human being going to hell than we are about what they will think of us, what they will say, or what could happen to us physically as a result of witnessing to them.

I think this can only be accomplished through God's Word, His sanctification process, and learning from other emotionally mature Christians. It will never be learned from immature parents, immature leaders, or immature preachers. I absolutely despise how cheap "grace" has become in mainstream Christianity. It is also bewildering to see how some Christians love to be defined by negative sinful moods. One person may be known as the sarcastic one in the church, the one you have to tiptoe around because he could explode in anger at the drop of a hat. Another may be known as the "horny" or sexually aroused one—which occurred recently in one of our youth groups.

Why do we glory in sin that should be to our shame? We should never be comfortable with sinful aspect in ourselves. For members of God's church, the impact of emotional maturity on our spiritual lives is of the utmost importance, because control of our emotions directly affects our spiritual maturity.

This can be easily seen by breaking down what Satan does and what God does. Satan takes; God gives. Satan hates; God loves. Satan comes to kill, steal, and destroy; God gives everything, creates, renews, loves, and even rebuilds. Satan does everything for himself; God goes above and beyond for us. We need to let this shape our thinking about whom we will yield our feelings and emotions to.

A different aspect of emotional maturity that we Christians definitely need to learn is not to let anything and everything affect us. When someone treats us mean, do we have to get angry or hurt? When someone is successful in life, do we have to get jealous or let envy control us? Even though we are overwhelmed with a sexually charged culture, do we have to let lust or sexual fantasies control our thoughts, feelings, and behaviors?

Why can't we look past the angry or mean person and try to find out *why* they are so angry and mean, to pray for them and shower them with love, no matter how many times they are mean to us? Why do we not share in the joy of people who are successful, or work on killing jealousy in our hearts and minds? Why do we not go to extreme lengths to kill access to sexual fantasies, and get help when needed?

I know this is hard, but God wants us to function this way. He wants us to have a great witness while here on this earth. He commands us to act, feel, and think certain ways. Is that a hard pill to swallow in this day and age? You bet it is. We need to rise above immature thoughts, feelings, and behaviors, though. We will have more emotional stability if we do.

This whole concept of emotional maturity makes me think of a story my dad likes to tell. It was what happened one day between my older brother and myself.

One day my brother and I were both playing in the sandbox outside. My father had just finished working on some piece of farm machinery and had gone into the house for a drink of water. As he drank his glass of water, he watched us through the kitchen window. He noticed that we were fighting, and he was fixing to come outside and put a stop to it when he saw me walk away. He thought the matter was resolved and was turning to leave the window—when he happened to see out of the corner of his eye that I was getting a small metal shovel. To his horror, he realized by the look on my face that I was going back to the sandbox, shovel in hand, to take out my anger on my brother who was turned the other way and would never see what was coming. He dropped his drinking glass in the sink and flew out of the house. He says he managed to reach me while I was in mid-swing and so prevented brain damage to my brother.

Taking a look back, I realize that I was upset and hurt by whatever we were fighting about. I wanted to feel better by hurting my brother. I let anger, frustration, rage, or whatever other emotion was going through my head at the time take control and almost lead to disastrous results. We as Christians must stop acting like this. It is usually not as dramatic as shovel-bashing whoever hurt us, but what we do still has devastating results. Whatever way we choose to get back at someone—by holding a grudge, spreading gossip, hating them, or any other thousands of sinful ways we can treat someone—it is just wrong. We will still end up with a hurt witness or a broken relationship.

We need to have a witness that demands notice. When our feelings and reactions to things are so different from the way the world feels and reacts, people won't be able to understand why we act and feel the way we do. And then they will ask others—or us—the *how*, *why*, and *what*, trying to figure out why we are the way we are. It will be wonderful, then, to be able to give them the answer for why we have the hope that we do. Our answers can be as simple as "Jesus Christ," our own personal testimonies, or whatever the Holy Spirit may impress upon you to say at that time.

The bottom line is that you react, feel, and behave so differently from the world because you are a Christian. We do not need to be waiting to bash someone with a shovel.

The second step toward emotional stability is to have *emotions* without *emotionalism*.

In Ecclesiastes 3, the author talks about a time for everything. Ecclesiastes 3:4, 8 say that there is "a time to weep and a time to laugh, a time to mourn and a time to dance . . . a time to love and a time to hate."

Is there anything wrong with having emotions or feelings at the proper time? No! Don't let anyone tell you otherwise.

If I was your friend and happened to meet you after one of your best friends or a dearly loved family member had died, I would expect you to be in mourning. If you were singing songs and dancing around on that day, I would naturally have concerns. Why? Because grieving is only natural when we lose a loved one, even if we know that loved one has gone to heaven.

As Christians we can have real emotions, but *emotionalism* is something different. *Emotionalism* is when we let our emotions control us or just make us complete wrecks.

In 1 Corinthians 9, we have Paul's description of running a race and disciplining himself like an athlete. I believe this translates well into our world of emotions and feelings. We can discipline ourselves to keep our emotions from running us. As Christians, we need to keep anger and bitterness from turning us into perpetually grumpy people.

We can do this by unloading our problems, issues, and concerns on God in prayer. We can do this by forgiving other people, even when they are the ones who have wronged us. Does that need to be repeated?

Wouldn't that be an emotionally mature aspect of our Christian life and a great witness to everyone in general, if we forgave and loved those who wronged us? Instead of holding on to the anger and bitterness, we can let it go and let God and His Word shape our feelings and actions. Are we not commanded to act like this in Scripture as well? If you are wondering whether we are, the short answer is *yes!*

When tragedy happens in our lives, and after a time of real emotions, we can react differently by seeing how we can grow or what we can learn from the experience. God may be using that time in your life for something He wants you to do as a result of it.

I love the stories of Christians who have experienced the love of God during the death of a loved one. They often share about how God came down in a very real way throughout the ordeal or at one specific time to overwhelm them with love or assurance, letting them know that He was right there beside them or that He was the first to feel their pain. Some have even led other family members or friends to belief in Christ during these times. This takes an emotionally stable and mature person who can step back during a time of grief or great emotion and focus on kingdom work instead of themselves.

I love to hear stories of Christians who praise God in the middle of dying from cancer. They don't know why they are going through what they are going through, but they endure it with such peace, joy, and showering of love to those around them that the lost and Christians alike are amazed. It is awesome that these Christians do not sink into a deep, dark depression, don't blame God, and use the time they have left on this earth to honor, glorify, and testify about our God. All of us who call ourselves Christians should strive to be like that.

If we do not think or act like this, we might end up like Job. If you want to keep asking God *why* at different times in your life, you had better be ready for the answer He might give. He might answer with love and understanding, or He might answer with anger. He might answer you with a challenge. He might answer like He did in Job 38:1-4: "Then the Lord answered Job out of the storm. He said: 'Who is this that darkens my counsel with words without knowledge? Brace yourself like a man; I will question you, and you shall answer me. Where were you when I laid the earth's foundation? Tell me, if you understand.'"

We will not understand everything in this life. Sometimes we understand things while going through them; sometimes it's not until afterward. Some things I don't think we will understand until we mature more in our knowledge of God or we are in heaven with God. (But then I wonder if we will even care once we are in heaven, praising and living in the glory of our God forever.)

I do know that we will get off track in this Christian life if we always want answers and reasons for everything. God will sometimes answer us, and we need to be ready to be astounded by the answers. Most of the time, the answers God gives to our prayers and the reasons for why things happen are different from what we expect or think. We just need to resolve to continue to praise Him and put our faith, trust, and hope in Him. But if you want to keep asking, questioning, blaming, and/or telling God all about what you think of the situation, then be ready for a Job 38 answer.

You are not God, and you never will be. His ways and thoughts are higher, better, and unbelievably more complex than ours. He may have pointed you out to Satan as an example of how awesome a Christian you are—and then let Satan destroy everything valuable in your life. Will you continue to praise Him and trust Him? Or will you fall into sinful thinking, feelings, and actions that lead to sin and to Satan winning a heavenly showdown?

In closing, I would like to share a time in my life when I let my feelings get the best of me. It was during our life as a young married couple at seminary. While there, I went to school full-time and worked full-time. This resulted in a very tired husband at the end of the day. To add to the stress, we already had one daughter, and were blessed with two more children during seminary. I was about halfway through seminary when I really started to feel burned out. Going to school, then immediately going to work, having a little family time when I got home, and then doing homework until all hours of the night—this was how my days went. It just seemed to repeat day after day.

At the beginning of seminary, it was exciting to be so busy and learning so much. I remember that a lot of us married students who had to work would joke about how crazy our lives were, and it seemed like we almost gloried in our stressful and hectic schedules.

One late night while working on homework at the computer, I was feeling extremely stressed-out. I gave in to all the feelings of hopelessness I had ever felt about seminary. I thought about how some of the other guys didn't seem to have it so hard or even have to work so much. So, why did I? After dwelling on negative thoughts and feelings for a while, I decided I should read my Bible to try to get out of the pit I was in.

I had been reading in Hebrews for some class, and I decided to just keep reading. I came to the great chapter of faith in Hebrews 11, and I was happy because I knew that if anyone needed some encouragement in faith, it was me. I was reading and got stuck on Hebrews 11:13-16 that reads:

> All these people were still living by faith when they died. They did not receive the things promised; they only saw them and welcomed them from a distance. And they admitted that they were aliens and strangers on earth. People who say such things show that they are looking for a country of their own. If they had been thinking of the country they had left, they would have had opportunity to return. Instead, they were longing for a better country—a heavenly one. Therefore God is not ashamed to be called their God, for he has prepared a city for them.

My eyes fixed on the words: *If they had been thinking of the country they had left, they would have had opportunity to return.* I started pondering about where I'd left and where I'd grown up. I'd lived my whole life on a farm in Oklahoma, and now I was in the big city in Texas. In thinking about the farm where my dad worked so hard, I realized that I could go home and help him. As much as I disliked farm work, there were several positives about where I had been raised. I thought about the work ethic my kids could benefit from in growing up there, and how nice and peaceful it was on the farm. I cast aside everything negative about going home and concentrated and how good it would be to get out of the big city and the crazy environment of seminary. I almost ran to my wife to tell her how awesome it was going to be to get out of where we were.

While going down the hall to our room, the door burst open, and there my wife was carrying a huge load of laundry. She reminded me that the washers and dryers were empty at this late hour and asked if I would carry the load down to the laundry room in the middle of the apartments for her. Honestly, I was not very happy to help her, because it was just one more thing I had to do. While walking back to our apartment after dropping off the first load, I was thinking that if we moved back to Oklahoma I wouldn't ever have to do this again, because we would have a washer and dryer in our house. Then something happened that I don't think I will ever forget; I still remember it crystal-clear to this day.

I felt God's presence come down and stop me halfway up the stairs to our apartment. The impression He laid on my heart was that I was at a *big* crossroads in my life. Mentally, I saw two paths laid out before me. I felt God saying, *You can go down either path; it is your choice. On one path means going home and working for your dad on the farm. You can have all the joys that will come with that. On the other path is My will and plan for your life. It will be harder than you can imagine, but it is my plan. Stop whining and complaining. Am I not here with you? Have I not provided for you? Pick a path, and stop waffling and entertaining thoughts that divide yourself. You know which one I want you on, but go home if you are only going to be grumbling and complaining for the rest of your time here.*

After the laundry was done, I went back and read that passage in Hebrews again. My eyes locked on the last verse, the one that says, "Instead they were longing for a better country—a heavenly one. Therefore God is not ashamed to be called their God, for he has prepared a city for them." I sat down and cried. I did not want God to be ashamed of me. I definitely wanted to long for a "better country" and not just go back "home." My definition of *home* changed that day. I committed my own and my family's life to make God first in it. Wherever He said *home* was to be, that would be where it was. Whatever he wanted me to do in my life, that was what I would do. I also made a commitment to stop letting my feelings control big decisions in my life.

It was a huge turning point in my Christian life. It was my first step in the direction of emotional stability and maturity. I could actually sing the hymn "Where He Leads Me I Will Follow" with a truthful heart instead of lying lips.

I hope we can all recognize the importance of feelings and emotions in our Christian lives. It is my prayer that you will be able to see the positives that come from feelings—and the dangers as well.

Never trust your feelings over the Word of God. Please, do not ever make decisions based on feelings; instead, make decisions only after much prayer and consulting with our living God.

If you think this is all nonsense, be prepared to feel miserable. If feelings rule your life, you will make decisions and do things that you will regret. This regret will only lead to being controlled more and more by feelings. You will remain in a vicious cycle of always trying to feel better by running to empty wells—whether they be drugs, alcohol, relationships, sex, money, status, fame, or whatever you want to fill in the blank with. Nothing will ever fill the void that only God's Word, the Holy Spirit, and Jesus Christ Himself can fill. There is rest and safety for your emotional well-being with God.

Make the change today. Trust Him with your feelings and emotions. He will handle them with care. Even if He deals with you in a seemingly harsh manner, it is only for your good. Our heavenly daddy loves us!

CHAPTER 5

Actions

They claim to know God,
but by their actions they deny him.
—Titus 1:16

The debate on the balance between *faith* and *works* (or actions) is still alive and well in the Christian church today. Is it faith and faith alone that saves you? Do works save you? Do a combination of faith and works save you? Does this stuff even matter?

In some churches, works are stressed as the highest level of concern for the Christian. In those churches, if you have no works or actions to go along with your faith, you do not really have any faith. They might even go so far as to tell people that if no works accompany your faith, then you are not going to heaven.

Other churches put little emphasis on works and actions and instead concentrate on building up knowledge, theology, and doctrine. In those churches, if you do not know the correct things about your faith, then you are looked at as foolish. The church might do some good things, but the majority of believers have lives without works, because the focus is on knowing, learning, and teaching. They never get to the "doing" part.

Before we dive into this deeper, I must confess something to you: I love Bible commentaries. It is amazing to read insights of individuals who lived three hundred years ago—or fifty years ago—and from the great Bible teachers of today. It also amuses me that I can argue with someone who has been dead for three hundred years. At times I cannot believe how a commentator can get one verse so "right" and then, two verses over, seemingly lose his mind. However, I am humbled when I realize that I am guilty of the same errors when the Holy Spirit comes in and gives me a fresh revelation from Scripture that proves I was misguided or ignorant in my understanding of a certain passage.

Some of my favorite commentators are John MacArthur, Charles Spurgeon, William Barclay, and Matthew Henry. I like the free commentaries available on *E-Sword*.[3] Some Bibles with comments I enjoy are the *Life Application Study Bible*,[4] the *Scofield Study Bible*,[5] and the *New American Standard Study Bible*.[6] I am amazed when they have similar comments on the same Scripture. It is also very funny, amusing, frustrating, and challenging when they disagree vehemently with each other. At times it feels like I only look at what some guy thought because I know it is going to be wrong. Other times, I can get too comfortable with a favorite commentator and easily slip into wrong thinking about a certain passage, because I begin to put the commentator's opinion above the way God wants the Scripture interpreted. While attempting to formulate my thoughts about this chapter through much searching of the Scriptures, prayer, and reading of various commentaries, I found one that helped clear up my thinking on this age-old debate.

My grandfather gave me the *William Barclay Daily Study Bible Series*.[7] These books, printed in 1960, are worn, old, and show their age. I cherish them, partly because of the interesting and sometimes crazy way that Dr. Barclay gives commentary to the books of the New Testament, but mostly because I can see my grandfather's heart in his studies. There are underlined passages, disagreements, little notes written on the sides of pages, and reminders to use this or that story in an upcoming sermon.

---

[3]   See http://www.e-sword.net/downloads.html for download information

[4]   *Life Application Study Bible* (Grand Rapids: Zondervan, 2001).

[5]   *Scofield Study Bible* (New York: Oxford University Press, 2004).

[6]   *The Zondervan New American Standard Study Bible* (Grand Rapids: Zondervan, 1999).

[7]   William Barclay, *The Daily Study Bible Series* 2d ed. (Philadelphia: Westminster Press, 1960).

It still touches my heart when I come across a new underlined passage or a note that Grandpa wrote so many years ago.

You may be wondering what in the world this has to do with actions in the Christian faith. I think that Dr. Barclay does a wonderful job in addressing this issue. In his book, *The Letters of James and Peter*,[8] he provides insight into the faith versus works/actions dilemma in a way that I have never come across before.

Most people misunderstand the whole issue of faith and works. Most Christians and unbelievers get confused when they read certain passages of Scripture side by side. They end up thinking that the Bible is confused on this subject. They think that if Paul and James were to meet each other and discuss this issue, one, if not both of them, would leave with a black eye.

As always, the Word of God is very consistent on this issue. It is either lack of knowledge or lack of intelligence that keeps us from understanding these issues. Most Christians have not read enough of God's word—neither the New or Old Testament—to even formulate an educated opinion on the subject. Or if they have, they have not put time into meditating or studying it in order to understand it at a level that could solidify their thinking on the subject. This applies to many different areas of Scripture and issues that are discussed in the world today—not just faith versus works.

Dr. Barclay points out that what most people call the "Pauline" position could be summed up in Acts 16:31: "Believe in the Lord Jesus Christ and thou shalt be saved."[9] This results in some denominations and individuals believing and defending a "by faith only" view of salvation.

Then we have James coming along in James 2:14-25 and telling us how faith without deeds is dead. James 2:24 says, "You see that a person is justified by what he does and not by faith alone." This results in some denominations and individuals believing and defending a "saved by works" view of salvation.

---

8   William Barclay, *The Letters of James and Peter (The Daily Study Bible)* 2d ed. (Philadelphia: Westminster Press, 1960).
9   Ibid, 85.

Now we can see how putting Acts 16:31 and James 2:24 side by side could be a problem. However, one of the things we must learn as Christians is to never take a verse out of context and never stand on one verse in the Bible without reading the rest of it and gaining understanding on how God really feels about issues and the great themes that run throughout the Bible.

Dr. Barclay points out that the word *believe* in Acts 16:31 is not just a "purely intellectual" belief. Barclay explains that "to believe in Jesus was to take that belief into every part and section of life, and to live by it."[10] He also goes on to say, "It is easy to pervert Paulinism, and to emasculate the word believe of all effective meaning; and it is not Paulinism, but misunderstood or perverted Paulinism which James condemns. He is condemning profession without practice; he is condemning an intellectual acceptance of Christianity as opposed to an acceptance by the whole personality—and with that condemnation Paul would have entirely agreed."[11]

I wholeheartedly agree with this position. (As I hope you see, this kind of theme runs throughout every chapter in this book.) Being a Christian is about letting Jesus Christ be the Lord and King of your life. It should permeate every nook and cranny that is physically, mentally, and spiritually possible. Only a "fake," immature, or uneducated Christian would believe or think otherwise.

Dr. Barclay hit on one more aspect of this whole argument that I had never put together until I read it on my own. He says that there is one more difference between James and Paul. "And the main difference is this—*they begin at different times in the Christian life.* Paul begins *at the very beginning.* He insists that no man can ever win or earn the forgiveness of God; no man can ever put himself in the right relationship with God. That initial step must come from the free grace of God; a man can only accept the forgiveness which God offers him in Jesus Christ."[12]

Now let's go to where James begins: "James begins much later; James begins *with the professing Christian,* the man who already claims to have been forgiven, the man who already claims to be in this right

---

[10] Ibid, 86.
[11] Ibid, 85–86.
[12] Ibid, 86.

relationship with God. Such a man, James rightly says, must live a new life for he is a new creature. He has been *justified;* he must now go on to show that he is *sanctified.* And with that Paul would have entirely agreed."[13]

Here are a few more quotes out of the pages of Dr. Barclay's book. "The fact is that no man can be saved by works; but equally no man can be saved without producing works."[14] "We are not saved *by* deeds; we are saved *for* deeds."[15] "The one thing James cannot stand is profession without practice, words without deeds."[16] "It is not, as he sees it, a case of *either* faith *or* works; it is necessarily a case of *both* faith *and* works. It is all too true that people have a habit of presenting religion as an *either or,* but in every case it must be a *both and.*"[17]

As I look at the mess and fighting that come up between the different denominations over the theology and doctrinal beliefs on faith versus works in Christianity, I can learn a lot from Dr. Barclay's words. The characterization of a Christian life should be *change*—a change from former thoughts, actions, behaviors, and feelings to new thoughts, actions, behaviors, and feelings.

So why do we have Christians living no differently after supposedly "being saved," from the way they lived before salvation? Why do we have congregations that come to church every Saturday or Sunday, sit in the pews, praise God, and listen to a sermon, but then go out and live for the world the rest of the week?

Why do we have Christians who, when put side-by-side with unbelievers, show no difference in the *actions* and *deeds* they do throughout their lives?

This is to our shame as believers if we fall into any of these negative categories. You need to take a long hard look in the mirror if there are no actions, deeds, or behaviors that back up your profession that you are a Christian. These things should overflow out of the Holy Spirit that lives inside of you. Only love for this world, caring more about what

---

13   Ibid, 87.
14   Ibid.
15   Ibid.
16   Ibid, 88.
17   Ibid, 90.

people think than what God thinks, and sin keep us from living the life of a genuine, biblical Christ-follower.

Basic Actions/Deeds That Should Characterize Your Christian Life

This is not an exhaustive list; it could be that I miss some very obvious or vital ones. These are just ones that the Holy Spirit impressed upon me to write about.

Actions and Deeds for Others

This is where the outgoing concern for others, which should be evident in our Christian lives, is actually backed up with deeds that match that concern.

This subject should have a magnificent breadth, width, and depth to it. It can be as "easy" as helping an elderly person in any area of his life, giving to the poor, or seeing someone on the side of the road with a flat tire and offering to change it for them. It can be as "hard" as witnessing to a friend, coworker, or family member when God impresses you to do so.

The point is that we as Christians stop being *selfish*. When we finally surrender to the belief and understanding that this life is not about *us* anymore but about *Jesus Christ* and what He lived and taught—when we follow His example of being a servant to all—we will change our *actions* to match those *beliefs*.

When we take the focus off of *me* and shift it to *others*, God is smiling down on us from heaven.

My wife and I were married a couple of months after she completed high school. After living awhile in the small, junior-college town where we were both attending college, she gave me a compliment I still remember to this day. She said, "Honey, do you know that you have a great witness here?" At first I thought she was being sarcastic, and it kinda stung a little. When she insisted she was serious, I asked her to explain.

I was two years ahead of her in a small college where everyone knew everyone. When she met students and some professors that I'd already had, they would ask her if she was related to me or my cousin, who also went to the same college. She claimed that when she told them she was my wife, they would always say, "Oh, that's great; he's such a nice guy."

I had no idea that I was being nice—or anything else—to anybody. I am naturally an introvert, and I was way more introverted back then than I am today, so I thought I was pretty much keeping to myself most of the time. My wife explained that it wasn't anything special that I had done; it was just that I was "genuine" with people. The fact that I would talk to people, ask them how their day was—and really want to know how their day was—had made an impact on some of them. She said they told her that I was "bubbling out happiness and caring."

As I look back at that—realizing that I need to do a much better job of it today—I realize that it happened because I was letting all the love I was experiencing with God flow freely out of me. I had a mind-set of caring more about the people I encountered than about my priorities, worries, time demands, and how those things affected me. I wasn't letting my own self-centered tendencies choke out the Holy Spirit's ability to use me, so it had freedom to reign.

Shouldn't we as Christians be "bubbling" out joy, love, peace, happiness, kindness, goodness, gentleness, and any other fruit of the Spirit or trait that God wants us to be showing to others? This should be happening daily in our lives. Why do sarcasm, bitterness, despair, depression, anger, discontentment, and other negative characteristics seem to have so much control in our Christian lives?

Let God, His Word, and the Holy Spirit change your mind-set and your actions into a focus on *others*. It will change the way you do things, but it will be for the infinitely greater good.

Actions and Deeds That Shine

These are works that shine out so believers and unbelievers alike can see them. The end goal of these deeds is to point others to Jesus Christ.

A word of caution before we dive into this one. Does this mean we purposely do things so everyone can "look at me"? Does this mean that we go out of our way to get noticed by others? No!

These actions, works, or deeds are never done from any kind of prideful or self-centered mind-set, attitude, or reasoning. If they are, you'll fall into one of Satan's clever traps and be forever seeking recognition and approval for what you do. Instead of giving *God* all the glory and credit, you will want the praise and applause to come *your* way.

God takes this *very* seriously. Just read Acts 12:21-24 if you doubt the seriousness of not giving God his due and wanting praise for yourself. He killed Herod because of it. I don't think almighty God has changed His opinion on this. Remember, just because grace, love, and mercy are being extended today does not mean that judgment is not coming. It is coming, and it could be tomorrow that it comes. Let us live today as Christ-followers who shine out for Him, giving Him all the glory, honor, and credit, so that we will not be ashamed of the way we lived when we stand before Him in the end.

Now that we covered that, let's contemplate some verses—just in case you think that James is the only book in the Bible to take a serious view of actions and works.

"Dear children, let us not love with words or tongue but with *actions* and in truth" (1 John 3:18, emphasis mine).

"Live such good lives among the pagans that, though they accuse you of doing wrong, they may see your good *deeds* and glorify God on the day he visits us" (1 Peter 2:12, emphasis mine).

"I tell you the truth, anyone who has faith in me will *do* what I have been *doing*. He will *do even greater things* than these, because I am going to the Father" (John 14:12, words of Jesus, emphasis mine).

"My mother and brothers are those who hear God's word and put it into *practice*" (Luke 8:21, words of Jesus, emphasis mine).

"I tell you the truth, no servant is greater than his master, nor is a messenger greater than the one who sent him. Now that you know these things, you will be blessed if you *do* them" (John 13:16-17, words of Jesus, emphasis mine).

If John, Peter, and, most importantly, Jesus have strong views and obvious feelings about actions, works, and deeds, don't you think Christians today should follow their examples?

It is an important step in your Christian sanctification and growth process to live out actions and deeds in this life. It does not matter how uncomfortable those actions make you feel. It does not matter if you have never done some of them before. What does matter is that you live out what you intellectually and verbally say you believe. Your belief and faith go hand-in-hand with your actions, works, and deeds. They do not exist independently. If they do, you are likely to have serious problems in your Christian life.

In closing, think about what would have happened if Christ had followed God's will the way many Christians today do. What if His actions were like the actions and deeds of Christians today? It makes me shudder and feel broken.

What if Jesus had decided it was too hard to go through the act of being the sacrificial Lamb for the world? What if Jesus had become fed up with all the sinners, hypocrites, and faithless followers? What if He had gone back to His Father, hopeless, dejected, and despairing because of the trials, suffering, persecution, and unbelief He was confronted with? What if Jesus had given in to the temptations and offers Satan confronted Him with?

Contemplating this should have us trembling and thinking about how truly awesome, heroic, magnificent, and persevering Jesus was and is.

Never forget that we have an awesome Savior! We have a great High Priest! He is still interceding on our behalf, which means that He is still doing awesome and wonderful *works* for us. And He is coming back one day!

You will have a pretty worthless and superficial life for God's kingdom if your beliefs and faith are never accompanied by sacrificial, loving, or refining actions.

You have a misguided faith if your deeds are done only for your own desires and priorities instead of being based on God's Word and the direction the Holy Spirit and God want you to take while you are here on this earth.

Live for Christ and be defined by actions for Him and for others. Why do any less? He gave and did so much for you.

You say you love Him, but what good is saying it if you never follow it up with actions?

CHAPTER 6

Spiritual Warfare

The first step on the way to victory
is to recognize the enemy.
—Corrie Ten Boom

For some Christians, the title of this chapter is offensive, while others will read this chapter first because of the excitement associated with the topic. There are Christians who are obsessed with talking about every aspect of spiritual warfare they can think of, while others remain firm in never talking about spiritual warfare, because they do not believe it exists in this day and age. I would urge a balanced approach to the topic of spiritual warfare.

I am reminded of a sermon I heard from Paige Patterson. It was memorable because the prop he used to make his sermon points was a double-barreled shotgun. I cannot remember if he loaded real shells into the gun or not, but just having the gun at the pulpit was an image I will remember forever.

He preached about two dangers that come when talking about such things as Satan, demons, and spiritual warfare. His first point was that a Christian can spend too much time studying, becoming involved in, and thinking about spiritual warfare, demons, and Satan. He cautioned that this sometimes results in falling prey to demonic forces and Satan's planning.

The second point he brought out was that it is also dangerous to just ignore everything about Satan, demons, or spiritual warfare. If we ignore or pretend like they don't exist, it is just as dangerous as the other extreme. Both points—or bullets, as the imagery went—can kill a Christian.

I had heard sermons like this before, but never with such visual clarity and good Scriptural exposition. (I should mention here that this memory is coming from the fallible human mind of the author. If the sermon had been videotaped and we watched it today, those might not be the exact words Dr. Patterson said or the points he made. So I apologize to him if those were not the points he was trying to get across to the audience. I am just sharing the gist of the message the way I remember it.)

I have to agree with Dr. Patterson; we must have balance in approaching spiritual warfare and subjects such as Satan, demons, and other topics along those lines. Unless God calls you to become the foremost expert on demons, Satan, and spiritual warfare, I would watch how much time you spend studying such things. If you are a young or immature Christian, I would advise not studying such subjects extensively or at all. Just know what the Word of God says about such things, and meditate on those passages.

On the other hand, should a mature believer be afraid of studying or teaching on such subjects? By all means, no! I remember hearing of a church that stopped a Bible study on demons and Satan because "things" started happening. (They were probably headed down the right track if Satan started messing with them in visible ways.) They stopped the study because they were afraid to continue it.

It is hard to describe what is going on in Christianity today in the realm of spiritual warfare. When I look around at the majority of Christians, it seems like most are ignoring this area. There are so many areas where Satan is obviously winning. Homosexuality, abortion, pornography, our insatiable materialism, addictions of all shapes and sizes, and television content are just a few of the many areas where Satan is alive and well. We have churches and denominations that endorse homosexual leaders and ministers or have practicing abortion doctors on staff. Entire churches are consumed with materialism and only produce more materialistic followers. Many do not care what kinds of things we or our children watch on TV.

Where has our love of truth in the Word of God gone? Do we care more about being politically correct than we do about proclaiming and holding steadfast to the Bible and the principles of God? Are we asleep as Christians, just letting Satan win in any area he chooses to kill, steal, or destroy? Have Christians just turned numb to the powers of darkness, because everywhere they look they find some wrong or sinful aspect in our culture? Have we just given up?

Sadly, I realize that there are misled, confused, ignorant, or even "fake" Christians who will read the previous couple of paragraphs and have problems with them.

I could quote Psalm 139:13-14, which reads, "For you created my inmost being; you knit me together in my mother's womb. I praise you because I am fearfully and wonderfully made; your works are wonderful, I know that full well," or Psalm 119:73a, which says, "Your hands made me and formed me." And even then, someone will still tell me that abortion is okay.

I could quote Romans 1:24-32, which tells us about how homosexuality came about in the first place, or Leviticus 18:22, a command from God himself that says, "Do not lie with a man as one lies with a woman; that is detestable." Even quoting those Scriptures or others like them will not change some people's minds.

Why? Because Satan is already winning the battle in their lives. They do not believe that God's word is one hundred percent true, one hundred percent accurate, one hundred percent valid, one hundred percent reliable, and one hundred percent authoritative. They have no faith to trust God at His word; they would rather believe this world and Satan's lies. They have no spine or fortitude to stand up for God, His Word, or any of His principles. Popular opinion, false research, and going with what feels good all rule their thoughts, minds, and decisions. Instead of honoring God, they would rather excuse away the way they believe with cries of "genetic predisposition" or "women's choice." The truth labels them murder, detestable acts, and abominations in God's eyes.

The truth in such people's minds is whatever pleases others, sounds good to the masses, or leaves them in position where they can never offend anyone by their personal opinions. These people are happy with their comfort zones, where everyone smiles after talking with them on such issues because they are so "well rounded."

If you are a new Christian who believes that homosexuality and abortion are okay because you haven't read enough Scripture to know better, then that is one thing. But if you are a Christian who rejects God's Word in favor of Satan's lies in order to please the world, then I hope you know that you are treading on dangerous ground.

When you start to pick and choose which passages of the Bible to believe, you are close to throwing it all away. Why? Because you don't know where your unbelief will stop or where you will draw the line about which Scriptures you will believe and which ones you will not. You will begin to go with what you "feel" to define truth or your beliefs, and you will break off, ignore, or reinterpret Scriptures that convict you or clash with the world's beliefs on how things should be.

It sickens me to see people who call themselves Christians go blatantly against God's Word, claiming it is because they are enlightened, and telling everyone how happy God is with them because of their level of understanding.

It infuriates me when those same "Christians" sit me down and explain to me why I can never stand up for or speak God's truth in a way that will offend someone or go against their pro-homosexual or pro-abortion stance. These people smile, with venom dripping from their lips, and inform me that the "conservative" Christian belief system is soon going to pass away.

I love to tell them how this isn't a "conservative" Christian stance I am taking; it is just the way every "normal" Christian should believe. Why? Because the Bible says so! It is the truth upon which we need to base all of our feelings, beliefs, decisions, thoughts, and actions. It is the only way we can start winning battles in spiritual warfare.

Now for some points about spiritual warfare that all Christians should be aware of.

SATAN IS GOING TO ATTACK YOU

"My prayer is not that you take them out of the world but that you protect them from the evil one" (John 17:15).

Jesus prayed this for his disciples near the end of his life. If Jesus prayed this for his disciples, shouldn't we take note of the importance of it? As Christians, we have to be concerned with being protected from the evil one. When we walk through this Christian life with no thought of our defense against Satan's schemes, we leave ourselves exposed.

As any good soldier would tell you, leaving yourself exposed to your enemy is a bad idea. It is hard to state in words just how bad an idea it is. So why do the majority of Christians leave themselves totally exposed and appear careless of the attacks of the enemy? I wish I could answer that in a satisfactory manner. The answers keep coming back the same, though. Ignorance of Scripture, lack of prayer, and absence of spiritual discipline or self-control in their lives are the obvious answers. Beyond those, I think, it is a matter of being unaware how relentless Satan is in his attacks against Christians.

I like to think of Satan as a wise general of evil. He is the epitome of evil, manipulation, trickery, and lies. He doesn't care about fighting fair, whom he hurts, or what tactics he has to use to destroy a Christian. When he and his legions of demons find something that can kill, steal, or destroy in any area of a Christian life, they go full throttle. Their intention is not nice at all.

I see some Christians giving in to Satan in areas that they think are harmless. These Christians are happily going down a path without seeing the end destination. Behind the scenes, Satan is working feverishly to keep the blinders on because, if these Christians could see the end of the path, they would run the other way as fast as their legs could carry them. At the end of the path is a dark room full of knives, ready and willing to cut the Christian apart. In this dark room is a lion waiting to tear the Christian's faith, hope, and trust in God to pieces.

In Satan's war room, it is his end goal to keep us from living, believing, and practicing the truth. However he can get his foot in the door of your heart, mind, or soul, he will do it. Satan's plan of attack is broad and powerful. Make no mistake about it!

Thinking of Satan as the greatest enemy coach has helped me in this area as well. All coaches from every sport watch videos and study their opponents. Satan and his top assistant-coach demons have watched an unbelievable amount of "video" on human beings since they were cast out of heaven. They know the weaknesses, failings, and avenues of temptations far beyond anything Bible scholars, writers, preachers, or professors will understand in their lifetimes. They know what weaknesses, failings, and avenues of temptations we will be prone to—probably before we do—just by studying us throughout our lives. Satan will have a well-prepared game plan to attack you, your family, your marriage, etc. Don't fall into the lie of thinking that Satan is powerless, feeble, or a dumb enemy. That is about as far from the truth as you can get.

(Don't think that I am building up Satan to be an unbeatable foe. We will get into that at the end of this chapter. I am just sick of naïve Christians falling into lies and temptations easily by thinking that Satan is a foolish and weak adversary.)

Satan's attacks can also be carried out over a long period of time. This reminds me of how I fell into sin and rebellion in my high school years. I was raised in a Christian household and was taught from a young age that sex before marriage, drinking alcohol, and taking drugs were wrong. My parents even hammered into my mind that hanging out or being friends with people who do those things was wrong as well. Looking back, I see a very sophisticated plan of attack that Satan employed—on my family first, and then using a personal plan that I went into happily and willingly.

The first part of the attack was in getting my family to stop having a daily Bible reading and prayer together. We had—for as long as I could remember—sat around the table at breakfast and read a little devotional and a few Bible verses, and then we would pray together. This disappeared sometime around the fifth or sixth grade.

I don't know why we quit; we just did. It was probably excused with many reasons—being too busy; thinking that my brother and I already knew enough Bible, since we went to church Sunday morning,

Sunday night, and Wednesday night; just simple human forgetfulness that turned into a habit of not doing it anymore; or any of a thousand reasons that caused us to stop doing this together as a family. The result from a spiritual perspective was a win for Satan. It stopped a download of truth and a quiet time with God every day in an adolescent boy's heart and mind. No one consciously said, "This is not important to us anymore." However, that was the result in my heart and mind when, a few years later, I jumped off the deep end into sin and rebellion.

The Bible and truth were not really important in my mind because we didn't read and pray together daily anymore. Was that a totally wrong excuse for me to sin? Yes. But it was the excuse I used. I don't blame my parents for my sins and rebellion that followed. I take full responsibility for them. However, I do wonder if things would have turned out differently if our family had not fallen prey to Satan's attacks that way.

The second part of Satan's multipronged attack was personal. It started with the slippery-slope tactic. The truths that I had held to on top of the mountain slope, I started to question.

All the thoughts and feelings about partying and sex before marriage that used to be set in stone started to crumble in junior high. I started idolizing the people in high school that did those things. Even though I knew they were wrong, I secretly wanted to try them and find out what I was missing. I still put on a good face at church and around my parents, but my thoughts were consumed with eventually participating in things like that.

Over the next few years, I went down the slope even more. I started hanging out with the party crowd and even went to a few parties. It was so exciting to be around beer, partying, and people who did that stuff. Even though I did not participate for a while, I got a big rush from just being around those things.

We all know what happens next, don't we? I finally gave in to the peer pressure to drink and go further than just kissing or holding hands with girls. The day it happened is still crystal-clear to me. I was in the field outside the town where I went to school, when I drank for the first time. What is even more clear than that is the words that a "friend" said to me when I was with him that day.

He looked at me with another one of our friends and said, "Man, we have been forever scheming on how to get you to do this with us. We were afraid you would quit being our friends if we asked you too many times. But this is so cool that you are doing this with us. Man, if only the people in town knew about this, they would freak out, and your family—wooooo, they would freak out! We won't tell; we won't tell. It's just so cool that you are with us now. We have been scheming and scheming for a long time on how to get you out here."

It honestly breaks my heart to look back at that and see Satan's plans so clearly—plans to get me to fall into temptation and sin. I can hear Satan or his demons in the voice of that friend so long ago—in the way that they had to plan to get me to stumble, the way they rejoiced in me finally being "with them," and the way we were glorying in what should have been our shame. It is painful to look back and see how easily I went into sin and temptation with my hands held out as if it were something good for me, something that I had been missing out on.

All it left me with was regret, lifelong consequences, and indescribable pain when I dwell on those things now as a maturing Christian. Even though it hurts, I am glad that God can reveal Satan's strategies through memories and experiences. Remember this:

- Satan will attack you.
- Whatever tactic he can use, he will use.
- If a certain tactic does not work, he will just switch to a new one.
- No matter how long it takes, he will be relentless in his plans.
- Wherever he can get you to loosen your grip on God's truth, he will, and then it is easy to fall down the slippery slope into sin, lies, and temptation.
- Satan's path of temptation, lies, and sin will be filled with bright lights, warm fuzzy feelings, and a "silver platter" of all our wants and desires. But the end of the path is a dark room full of knives and a lion waiting to cut you to shreds and tear you apart. His goal is the destruction of your Christian beliefs,

and actions that make you a useless, ineffective Christian.

SATAN WANTS YOU TO BE AFRAID

A. W. Tozer said, "We must meet the uncertainties of this world with the certainty of the world to come."

Does Satan care when you are afraid? No! He wants you to be afraid in any area of your life that will limit your ability to be a real and true follower of Christ.

One of the biggest fears you have to overcome is what others think of you as a Christian. This translates into every area of your life—what you listen to, how you talk, the activities you do for entertainment, how you witness to unbelievers, and how you shine your light for Christ. Whenever you draw a line in the sand—or the Holy Spirit convicts you to live a certain way—there is always in the back of our minds a fear of what others will think.

When the subject of music comes up in our lives, my wife and I unashamedly tell people that we listen only to Christian music. We feel that God has convicted us about the music we listen to and has shown us through many ways that listening only to Christian music benefits our family the most. This kind of view can bring mixed responses from unbelievers and believers alike.

We are told that we are narrow-minded and missing out on a lot of music that God has put in this world. We get asked, "Isn't that kind of boring and monotonous, always listening to the same type of music?" Sometimes we are told with smiles and condescending talk, "Well, I could never do that, but I guess whatever floats your boat." Other times we are happy to find other Christians who do the same.

The crazy part of all this is how our preferences in music can result in fear at times. We fear that we can't tell anyone how God has impressed us to live, because it might offend them. We question our convictions because of the fear that creeps in when we are not like the rest of the world. It is silly for us to feel muzzled or awkward around people when following something we believe in.

This is how Satan works with fear. Expand this thinking to almost any area in your Christian life, and see if Satan is not working behind the scenes to bring fear into it. He wants fear to freeze you, immobilize you, and capture your heart until you are too weak or afraid to live out any Christian beliefs, thoughts, feelings, or actions.

Think about why you do not witness as much as you should. It has a lot to do with the areas in which you have let fear become overwhelming. Is it because you are too scared of what other people will think of you? Are you more afraid of their reaction than you are concerned with sharing eternal, destination-changing information with them? The bottom line is that you have let fear overcome and control you. It is a selfish way to live as a Christian. When we are more concerned with how people will react, what they might say, how they might feel, or what they might do in response to our witnessing than we are about the fact that they will spend eternity in hell, forever separated from a God that loves them, it is a sad state for a Christian.

Do you not care about the Great Commission? In case you do not know, that is where Jesus commands and commissions us to do His work. How did we get to such a cowardly and sad position in our Christian life, where we care more about our own reputation, feelings, thoughts, and job security—or whatever excuse we comfort ourselves with for not being involved in a basic and vital part of Christianity?

Rise up, Christian! Join the fight for souls that is raging all around us! Do not fall into complacency or cowardice in any area of your Christian life! You are letting Satan win when you are sitting on the sidelines of the Christian life. Some people think of this as a safe place to be; it is not. God expects every Christian to be "in the game," so to speak. You don't have to ask the almighty Coach to put you in; you are already supposed to be having a vital role in the fight/game. When you asked Jesus to come into your heart, or made the decision to trust Him as your Savior, you were immediately thrust into the game, with or without knowing it.

Are you going to be a participating part of God's team? Or will you let Satan immobilize you and freeze you on the bench? It should be embarrassing for a Christian to be on the sidelines or the bench while the fight is raging in this world. Wake up, Christian! If you are on the sidelines and your feet are in chains because of the fear that Satan has overcome you with, wake up! Get in the game and start having a Christian life that is victorious rather than ineffective, selfish, and useless!

Also, do not give in to the fear of having to witness to everyone. Remember, if Satan finds out that one tactic does not work, it does not mean that he will quit or give up. He will just try another tactic. When he is unable to stop you from witnessing, he might overwhelm you with the thought that you need to save everyone you come across in your life. This results in a paralyzing fear that overwhelms us.

In reality, God wants us to be open to witnessing to anyone He impresses on our hearts to witness to. We must always be ready to "give a reason for the hope we have within us," but don't let that freak you out. Ask God for "divine appointments." Always keep an attitude of being open and ready to be used by God at any time. It does not matter what time of day, who it is, how long or how many times it takes. Just be ready to witness.

Whenever, wherever, and *whoever* would be a good mind-set to have about witnessing. God does not expect you to save or witness to everyone on the planet. God does expect you to be open to witnessing to anyone, though.

When we think about it that way, the fear dissipates a little. Even though you may still let fear creep in when thinking about talking to a complete stranger, workplace associate, or family member about Christ, don't let it make you give up. The words of Jesus should give us resolve, courage, fortitude, and strength to overcome it.

Do not let any fear from Satan defeat you. Remind Satan where he is going to spend eternity—in the eternal lake of fire forever and ever. I have fallen into temptation and been led astray by Satan numerous times, which has resulted in hurt, broken, or wrong feelings, thoughts, and actions, and I love to be able to return the favor. I think it makes him mad and strikes fear in his heart when I remind him where he is going for eternity and where I will be for eternity. I will get to be in a place of eternal happiness, love, and rest beyond my comprehension. He will be tormented, in agony, and in a place of condemnation forever. Try this; it always brightens my day.

SATAN OPERATES WITH A SENSE OF URGENCY

Satan only has a limited time to continue doing business. Every day brings us one day closer to his certain demise. This naturally makes him and all the dark forces and powers of the earth work harder, faster, and more brutally as the end draws near.

We can see this played out in Scripture as well. In Revelation, we see the dark forces, the Antichrist, and Satan having more power (or at least it is displayed more openly) than perhaps anytime in the history of the universe. May we never forget that God allows him to have this power. Unfortunately, many fake and superficial Christians will be tricked by the signs and wonders Scripture speaks of and be all too eager to switch allegiance to what they can see and experience right in front of them, instead of trusting and relying on faith.

Now I have a warning—and comfort—for the Christian who is following God's will at the present time. Satan will only heighten his attacks against you now and in the future. When you are truly following God's will, Satan hates you, and you move up to Number One on his Most Wanted list. He will fight with unparalleled viciousness and hostility to keep you from continuing down the straight and narrow. Instead of letting fear creep in or giving up entirely, *stand firm on God's word and pray all the harder.*

It sickens me to think how little we fight against him at times. It disgusts me how many men I personally know that have given up on ministry life, marriages, families, and jobs they know God has called them to do or commanded them about, all because they have fallen prey to Satan's lies, temptations, and attacks.

Do not be a casualty of war. Be a soldier in it. Have some victories in this spiritual war. If I could show you how scarred, dented, and rusty my spiritual armor is and has been, I would. Don't let discouragement take control when you fall or fail. Gain insight from the scars and dents in your armor, and don't let Satan win in those areas any more. Draw strength from all the times you've been knocked down, because at least you have gotten back up to stand again. We are supposed to be in this fight; we are supposed to be maturing and learning from our previous battles; and we should be coming to a sense of familiarity with the different pieces of our spiritual armor. (Ephesians 6 is where you will find information on the different pieces of your spiritual armor as a Christian.)

Gain a sense of urgency about your spiritual life. Remember that every day is a gift from God and that you are not promised tomorrow. If you were to die today, would you be happy or content with how you have lived your life up until now? If you were to die today, would you only be ashamed and convicted about how you've lived your life up until now? These are questions you should not be afraid to answer. Satan is winning if you have no urgency for godly matters in your life.

MY OWN EXPERIENCES WITH SPIRITUAL WARFARE

This next section is hard for me to share because of the way I was raised. In my family and the church I grew up in, it was rare and uncomfortable to talk about Satan, demons, or spiritual warfare. Nobody in the church disagreed on whether or not Satan was real; it was just a topic that was seldom talked about. Even today, if the subject comes up too much, people begin to say things: you are either consumed with the subject, or you are a freak because you believe in such things. I think this happens in many churches. So, if you start to talk about any of your own experiences with fellow Christians, be prepared for mixed responses. They might identify with you and then have great conversations about it. They might respond with bewilderment and advise you to check into a mental institution. They might advise you to be silent because you are going to upset someone. They might tell you that those things do not happen, so you should quit telling lies. Be prepared for these responses, because I know I sure wasn't ready to handle Christians' reactions to our experiences. Those stories are probably best left for another time.

Ever since I gave my life to Christ on that mission trip, I began to notice a change in how I processed things in my mind. I started to recognize when Satan was speaking, tempting, and trying to lead me astray as opposed to the Holy Spirit convicting, enlightening, or leading me down the straight and narrow. This was a big change, since I had previously based decisions on my own desires, whims, and passions. Like a Jedi from Star Wars, I noticed that there was a difference between the light side of the force and the dark side of the force. There was truth that came from God, which resulted in holy and righteous thoughts, feelings, and actions. On the opposite side there were lies that came from Satan, which resulted in sin-filled thoughts, feelings, and actions.

The first time I really felt spiritually attacked was when my wife and I went to Colorado to tour college campuses where I might become a director of a campus ministry. We were driving around one particular campus and praying that God would reveal to us if this was the campus where He wanted us.

While touring the campus, I kept getting bombarded with certain thoughts in my mind: *You are a loser! What are you doing out here? What possible good could you do, loser? You could never be a good campus minister! Why waste your time? This isn't the place for you!* On and on came thoughts of how bad a job I would do, what a loser and failure at life I was, how my past sins and failures made me unqualified, and just what a waste of time it would be to try to start up a campus ministry at a college where there was not one at all.

After the tour, my wife and I went out to lunch. Before we prayed over our meal, my wife asked me if God had revealed anything to me. I shared the feelings and thoughts that were weighing down on me. She told me she had wondered what was wrong with me, because I had walked around the campus with a sad face the whole time. I was not even aware of it. Then she told me something that we still remember to this day. She told me that she didn't think God would talk to me that way and that it had to be Satan.

I was so wrapped up in those thoughts and feelings that it was remarkable to me that she'd said it. It was like a lightbulb went on in my head, and I thought, "Yeah, He wouldn't do that, would he?" I thought about what an idiot I had been for letting it affect me so much. We talked and ended our lunch with strong prayer against Satan and any forces of darkness that were attacking us. During that prayer, I literally felt an oppressive weight taken off of my shoulders and chest. It was like I could breathe freely again. I was amazed—and a little scared.

Later that day, I felt God finally speak and impress upon my heart. He informed me that He was not going to tell me if this was the college He wanted us to minister to. He wanted me to know that Satan was alive and well in the community in which the college was located. He also wanted me to know that the college itself was a demonic stronghold and that I was going to have to step up and be a soldier if I was going to minister there. He impressed upon my heart that He would be happy for us to work there, but I needed to know it was going to be a fight, and spiritual warfare was going to take place. He ended it with a challenge that went kind of like this: *If you come here, it will be hard. They will fight against the truth of my Word; they will hate you for your love of my Son; you will be attacked; you will be hurt. But will you come and serve Me here?*

I accepted it and shared it with my wife. And we both accepted the call.

Months later when we moved out to Colorado, our first "scary" spiritual attack happened. It was during the first few weeks, and we were at home one night. We had gotten our kids to sleep, and then we were just sitting around talking—when someone banged on the door. I went and answered the door, but nobody was there. I thought nothing of it, until it happened a few more times. I got kind of upset, thinking it was kids that we didn't know in the neighborhood we lived in. So I crouched by the door, just waiting for the next knock to happen, and when it did I was going to jerk open the door and scare the kid silly to teach him a lesson.

I waited for a while and had just decided to sit down, when the banging knock happened. I sprang up and wrenched open the door, all in one motion. I was very surprised to greet only empty night air. I rushed around the side of the house and did not see anyone. I even spent time looking for tracks and could not find a single track in the snow. I started to get a little scared, and so did my wife. I did what any good country boy would do; I got my shotgun and waited for it to happen again.

The next banging that came was on the roof. I jumped outside and was ready to shoot whatever or whoever was on the roof, but there was nobody there. I came back inside, and my wife had the phone in her hand ready to dial 9-1-1. The banging knocks continued on the side of the house, the roof, and the front door. All the while, I was running around with my twelve-gauge shotgun, trying to figure out what was going on. I was just glad the kids did not wake up and see their dad during that time and think he was as crazy as a loon.

It finally occurred to me that the source could be spiritual, and that was when I felt a pure sense of evil sweep through our living room. We decided to pray, and after a while the sense of evil left, and there were no more instances of banging anywhere in the house. It really shook me to my core, because I had never been trained or taught how to deal with things like this. I really thought we must have been losing our minds and tried to find "logical" explanations of why this would happen.

A few days later, God gave me an answer during prayer time. He explained to me that it was demons that were trying to scare us and get us to leave. They didn't like us or what we were trying to do at the college. I was surprised and honestly scared, and I wondered why God would let this happen. He gently reminded me that He had already told me that we were going to be attacked, and He asked me why I was so surprised when it actually happened. I felt really silly and admitted that He was right. I resolved not to be frightened by anything like that in the future—and to be encouraged if anything like that happened again.

Things were quiet for a while. I was so involved and consumed with ministry life that there was no time for anything else. I was reading my Bible and having a good quiet time every day. It wasn't until a year or so had passed that I started to neglect reading my Bible or having serious prayer time with God. I think this failing relates directly to the frequency of spiritual attacks. Although it is not always the case, the more time I spend with God in prayer and personal Bible reading, the less frequent and less powerful it is when Satan and his forces attack.

DREAMS

This is where Satan seemingly moved to and still attacks me to this day. I'm a vivid dreamer, and that does not help.

It started after I got hurt on a skiing trip with several college students. I shattered my collarbone and had to get a plate put in with eight screws so I would have a functional shoulder. I slept in our living room on our comfortable recliner, because lying flat on the bed was way too painful. In my dream, I "woke up," and the lighting was exactly the same as it would have been if I had opened my eyes in real life.

I heard my kids screaming, and I could not get up out of the recliner because I was tied to it. They were being tortured, and these deepest-black beings came and told me that they would stop it if I would leave Colorado or just renounce my beliefs in Jesus Christ. I took exception to that, and since I couldn't do anything else, I started singing hymns. "On Christ the Solid Rock I Stand" was a chorus I kept singing and yelling repeatedly. They really didn't like that. So the screams intensified, and they told me I would be the reason that my kids died in agony. I just kept singing, while angry and agonized tears flowed down my face. Enraged and seemingly desperate, they choked me until I blacked out. I woke up and had actual tears coming down my face. I could not believe that it had not really happened until I saw that my kids were fine.

There were variations of this kind of dream, and through prayer God started giving me interpretations of the dreams. I felt like Daniel, getting the interpretation from God and then telling my wife or someone else about it. It was uplifting and reassuring to get answers instead of just finding excuses not to go to bed and staying up at night with all the lights on in the house. That gets expensive.

I'll share a couple more dreams and their interpretations, and then we'll put this subject to rest.

One that my wife will remember forever happened about a year ago. In that dream, I was in my bed just exactly as I was in real life, and again the lighting was the same as when I opened my eyes. In this sequence of dreams, several demons kept coming into my room from the ceiling, under the bed, and through the door and kept trying to suffocate me with their bodies and hands. I usually wake up from these dreams when my wife shakes me or yells at me to wake up. In my dream, I realized that it was a dream and kept yelling and pleading for her to wake me up. I kept waking up in my dream, only to start over and find out it was a dream with demons attacking me. Finally, I guess I started actually yelling in real life, and my wife rolled over to wake me up as she has done countless times in our married life.

This time was different, though. As she rolled over, she said she saw an evil and demonic face on our ceiling trying to scare her. She hurriedly woke me up and turned on the light. I was surprised because, honestly, she is usually annoyed by my nightmares and having her sleep interrupted. She said she knew I was being attacked because of the sense of evil in our room and the crazy, demonic face she saw on our ceiling. She assured me that she would never be upset with my dreams again, since she had now seen and felt what I was experiencing in my dreams. The interpretation I got from God for that one was that the demons wanted us to be silent. We were sharing too much truth and were actually getting through to some of the college students that came to our meetings. God asked me if I was going to be silent. I answered no and then went out with a renewed strength and purpose on campus.

Another dream I will never forget happened after a time of having several demonic nightmares for an extended period of time. Every night I would pray for protection and deliverance from these kinds of nightmares. It seemed like God was not listening or answering at all. I could not understand why He would not remove them for me.

This dream started out with me watching from outside my house. All around my house were these giant-sized angels in splendidly bright armor. I could not really make out their features because of how bright they were. The light bursting forth from the angels shown in the darkness like the sun. I noticed that the roof of the house only came up to about their knees. Each of them held a huge sword in front of his face with both hands. They stood shoulder-to-shoulder, encircling the entire house. It seemed as if they were guarding our house, and the idea that I got was that they would completely destroy anything or anyone who tried to attack.

Then a completely unexpected thing happened. From behind our house, out of nowhere, came two little demons that were a little bigger than an average-sized dog. They walked right through the legs of one bright, shining angel and right through the window into our house. Then I was in my room, and the little demons came in and started trying to hurt me in my bed. I tried to get up but couldn't. I could move my legs, though. So I kicked them when they jumped on my chest and head to try to choke and suffocate me. Then they moved down and grabbed my legs and sat on them so I couldn't kick them.

When they did this, I started singing "Blessed Assurance," and this really made them mad. We went back and forth: I sang to them, then they jumped on my chest and face to try to silence me, and then I could kick them. Then they would jump back onto my legs, and I would go back to singing. This went on for quite a while, and I actually started laughing because of how comical the whole situation was. This *really* made them mad, and they switched to trying to cut me up with daggers they pulled out of nowhere. So I started yelling, which finally resulted in my yelling in real life and my wife waking me up.

The next day while driving around, I felt God impress upon me the interpretation of the dream. He told me that since I was whining, complaining, and feeling sorry for myself because He had apparently not answered my prayer, He decided to let me see into the spiritual world a little bit. The giant angels I'd seen were really there, protecting me from big attacks. Nothing big was going to hurt me or my family. They had been there since we arrived in Colorado, and they were not going anywhere.

Even though I felt unprotected, I was protected beyond my understanding or belief. The little demons symbolized that I was still going to encounter everyday spiritual warfare. God explained that they would always be trying to find new little ways to attack me, and it was up to me if I was going to let that stop me, silence my voice, or get me down in our ministry.

This really was an encouraging moment in my spiritual growth process. To know that we were protected was very stabilizing in the spiritual warfare area. I knew that there would still be attacks, but I was to look at them as insignificant when I saw how small they really were. The fact that I'd let things get out of proportion was my own fault. If I had let temptations, sin, or fear overwhelm me and turn into a big monster, it wasn't God's fault; it was mine.

The other dreams I have nowadays force me to watch my wife having sex with other people, to find her willingly cheating on me, to see our children not believing in Jesus, and to endure more variations of the old demonic dreams where they are attacking me. I know these are from Satan, but it is really crazy and juvenile how sometimes those dreams will affect me in real life. I sometimes wake up harboring bad feelings toward my wife because of the dream I had. It is crazy, but I guess if it works, that is why Satan hasn't stopped it yet. When I finally stop letting the nightmares affect me, I bet that Satan will order attacks in new areas of my life.

Another major area of my life that he attacks is my emotions. I have learned the hard way to depend on God and prayer for my emotional well-being.

I will not get into this very much, because it is still so real and raw in my life. Through my adolescent stupidity, I learned very well how to run to broken cisterns and empty wells to improve my emotional state. Whether I used alcohol, painkillers, or sexual sins, it really didn't matter, because those were the things I ran to with the assurance that happiness and peace would follow. Even when I knew that they would only lead to guilt, shame, and more pain, I couldn't have cared less, because I also knew beyond a shadow of a doubt that they would provide a temporary high and an escape from the pain, longing, and loneliness I was experiencing.

Perpetuating that cycle is about as stupid as we humans can get. Knowingly staying in something that will only provide more guilt, shame, and pain is confusing from an objective viewpoint, to say the least.

Why do we do it then? Because we have bought into the lie, directly from Satan, that we can get peace, happiness, and contentment anywhere . . . just not from God. It is sad but true. I know it breaks our Father's heart.

In closing, let me say that we can be vigilant in our efforts against Satan and his dark forces. We know that he loses in the end. Christians need to rise up and start living like we are the victors in this epic war. Our God is bigger, stronger, and infinitely more equipped to handle the Devil and anything he throws our way.

If you don't believe that, you either have God in a box or you have slipped into believing another of Satan's lies.

The next sections deal with how we overcome Satan.

RESISTING THE DEVIL

James 4:7 says, "Submit yourselves, then, to God. Resist the devil, and he will flee from you."

This is not a simple push-back. I like to envision the meaning behind this verse as putting up an extraordinary struggle. Satan comes to steal, kill, and destroy.

Imagine that you have all the money out of your checking and savings accounts and anything of worth in just one bag. What would happen if someone tried to take it from you? There would be a fight worthy of song and story, right? You would stop at nothing to make sure they did not get away with it. So, why don't we put up that kind of fight in our Christian lives? When we know there are sinful temptations beckoning to us, lies from Satan trying to overcome our Christian "common sense," or circumstances causing us to lose hope, faith, confidence in Christ, or trust in God, we need to *resist*! We need to stop letting Satan be the only lion in the world and turn and fight as ferocious Christian lions!

Why has your resistance in the past not always worked? Because you didn't mean it! You pushed Satan away with one hand while holding onto him with the other. You loved your sin more than you desired to become more holy and righteous. You were tricked by lies, or you willingly believed the lies, and you turned from God's truth whenever it was presented to you.

This verse will work if you remember that the resistance has to be an actual, true resistance. Imagine again, if you will, that someone is coming to kidnap your kids—or you, if you have no children. You know the kidnappers are only going to take you to a place of torture, agony, and death.

Will you willingly go with them or let them take your children? Of course not! You will fight with all your strength, and there will be no rules to the way you fight, either. You will use whatever works against the kidnappers to get away or to stop them, even if it means killing them to protect yourself or your kids.

This is the way it is with Satan's attacks. He will attack you, and He will follow no rules in His attack. Put up a fight! Don't use any rules in your fight against him. Get rid of sin in your life! Get rid of temptations! We can resist him, and he will *flee*!

Unfortunately, the majority of Christians do not believe this, or they certainly do not live like it. We are too well-acquainted, too comfortable with the sin that is killing us, and we excuse it away. We smile and tell ourselves that these little sins are not really affecting our spiritual lives. If only we could see the spiritual side of it, we would see great wounds and injuries covering us. From those wounds bleed our Christian beliefs, feelings, actions, faith, trust, and love. This renders us ineffective and unproductive Christians. It leaves us damaged, hurt, and in need of some divine restoration, reconciliation, and healing.

Don't buy into Satan's lies and games! Resist Satan, and he will flee. Get some victories under your belt in the battles against the dark forces ruling this world. Stand firm, knowing that God is with you, and Jesus Christ is mediating for you. Millions of Christians have gone before you and fought similar or worse fights, and millions more are out there fighting right now. *You are not alone.*

HAVING COURAGE

"But the Lord is faithful, and he will strengthen and protect you from the evil one" (2 Thessalonians 3:3).

Dictionary.com has excellent definitions of courage: "the quality of mind or spirit that enables a person to face difficulty, danger, pain, etc., without fear; bravery" and "have the courage of one's convictions, to act in accordance with one's beliefs, especially in spite of criticism."[18]

There are so many points that could come out of those definitions. I don't think we have enough time or paper, but I will say a few things about them anyway.

As Christians, we must have courage to face the difficult things in our lives. God wants us to overcome sin, ourselves, bad historical patterns, and temptations. He also wants us to follow Him wherever He leads. This will take a massive amount of courage and fortitude in

---

[18] http://www.dictionary.reference.com/browse/courage, accessed on September 7, 2011.

our lives. It will be hard but rewarding. It will be even more difficult when we know and realize that Satan will be around every corner and at every resting place, trying to mess us up.

In our Christian lives, we will also face danger. Satan will want you to chicken out or become overwhelmed by all kinds of real and perceived dangers. Will you? Or will you draw courage from God's word, Christ's example, and impressions by the Holy Spirit?

Satan will try to stop you from taking a step of faith off a cliff into thin air, so to speak, when God wants you to. He will fill your mind with fear, telling you that God will not catch you, saying anything that will stop you from taking the step or make you walk away from the cliff. This is sad when the result of taking the faith-step with God would have resulted in growing your faith, getting you closer to God, building your reassurance that God will catch you when you take that step, and becoming a stronger Christian overall. It takes courage to face danger in our spiritual lives.

Satan wants to attack you with pain as well. Courage in this area is paramount for your Christian life. Whether it is physical pain resulting from an accident or injury, spiritual pain, or physical and spiritual pain from the death of a loved one, Satan wants to use these things to kill, steal, and destroy any part of your Christian life that he can. He wants it to be the only thing you think about. He wants you to give in to the emotions and thoughts that come with dwelling on pain. He wants despair, hopelessness, and the sense that they will always be there to conquer your soul. We will need courage to war against these times.

Did Jesus lack courage when he was crucified or during the time that led up to the crucifixion? Many debate about exactly what He was feeling in the garden of Gethsemane. I think the debate should stop when we get to the actual scourging and crucifixion time, though. When the time came for it, He went willingly—without calling angels to help him, without using the power available to Him to blast the soldiers into pieces, and without crying or whining about it. That is courage that I can only aspire to have. I hope that I can be a sliver of how courageous our Lord, King, and Savior was. When faced with pain, we must have Christian courage.

We must have courage, without letting fear overcome us. There used to be value placed on bravery in this country. It still might be in places, but not to the degree that it once was. I think that translates to the church as well. There used to be value placed on Christians who spoke and lived in accordance with their beliefs. Now, in the United States especially, value is only placed on being politically correct and being able to please everyone with your words. Who cares what God's Word has to say? If you can please people and make them feel better, that is more important than God's Word today. As a person who is trying to lead his family and himself in being a true Christ-follower, this sickens me.

In the Bible, David and his mighty men are a great example of individuals who had courage and did not let fear overcome them. If you have not read the story of David and Goliath recently, read it again. It is found in 1 Samuel 17. Read David's words when he is talking to Saul and explaining his trust and faith in God, and especially when he is defying Goliath in 1 Samuel 17:45-47. Read about one of my favorites of David's mighty men, Benaiah, in 2 Samuel 23:20-23 and 1 Chronicles 11:22-25 for a mirrored account of his exploits. Benaiah went down into a pit on a snowy day and killed a lion. He also fought an Egyptian that was seven and a half feet tall. The Egyptian had a spear, and Benaiah only had a club—or a staff, as some translations and commentators disagree. Benaiah fought the Egyptian and ended up killing him with his own spear.

In my mind, it doesn't get any better than that—going into a fight with an inferior weapon and coming out on top by killing your enemy with his own weapon. And having the courage to go into a pit with a lion is some kind of courage, but on a snowy day—when your footing would be unsure, and movement would be difficult—this is courage on another level!

We Christians must draw from these examples to deepen and broaden our courage. In our battle against Satan, we are going to have to go down into a pit on a snowy day and kill some sin that we have become addicted to or entangled in. We must have courage, knowing that we are able to do things like this because of our confidence, trust, hope, and belief in God's power and the truth of His Word.

If we are going to live courageously in accordance with our beliefs—through our feelings, thoughts, and actions in the face of criticism—we are going to have to speak like David did to Goliath. Of course, our words are to be filled with love, but we need to have the heart of David. Whether it involves our own family members, people we work with, people in church, other Christians, or unbelievers, we must be able to courageously defend why we believe what we do and why we live the way we live.

God loves us and will always forgive us. But let's look into His mind to get a picture of how He views those with courage and those without—in case you haven't already got it cemented in your mind.

A coward is one who is without courage. I hope we all can agree on that point. Think about what happened to the Israelite nation after the twelve spies had made their report. They did not listen to the two courageous voices of Caleb and Joshua but instead listened to the cowardly voices and thinking of the other ten. The entire nation wandered in the desert for forty years until that cowardly and unbelieving generation died!

In Revelation 21, we also see what happens to the cowardly. First there is a speech by God, where He gives comforting words about giving us drink without cost and an inheritance in heaven—and about His being our God and us being His sons. After that, He says in Revelation 21:8, "But the *cowardly*, the unbelieving, the vile, the murderers, the sexually immoral, those who practice magic arts, the idolaters and all liars—their place will be in the fiery lake of burning sulfur. This is the second death" (emphasis mine).

Because "the cowardly" is mentioned in this list, I think we need to readjust our thinking in the Christian realm about cowardice. If you are not being courageous in your Christian life and are instead living as a coward, know that God takes this seriously. We are not supposed to be cowards; instead we are supposed to be courageous and to overcome whatever Satan or this world throw our way. We are supposed to overcome it.

Have courage in your Christian life. Know that Satan wants you to be afraid. Draw comfort from Scripture, and let it build courage in you.

In the book of Joshua, God is speaking to Joshua after the death of Moses. This is right before they cross the Jordan River to go into the Promised Land. I think this verse translates well into the realm of spiritual warfare. "Have I not commanded you? Be strong and courageous. Do not be terrified; do not be discouraged, for the Lord your God will be with you wherever you go" (Joshua 1:9).

"The one who is in you is greater than the one who is in the world" (1 John 4:4b). Our God is bigger, stronger, tougher, more powerful, and in control. Nothing happens without His knowledge, and He will not let Satan overpower you. He will not let Satan tempt you beyond what you can bear.

"Finally, be strong in the Lord and in his mighty power. Put on the full armor of God so that you can take your stand against the Devil's schemes" (Ephesians 6:10-11). Nothing less than the full armor of God will help you avoid becoming overwhelmed or falling prey to the Devil's schemes. You should probably do some research and meditation on what the full armor of God is and what it means. It can be found in Ephesians 6. Make sure that you have every piece in place. If you need to focus on working or polishing one piece of that armor, then get to work.

"Through the fear of the Lord a man avoids evil" (Proverbs 16:6b). If you have the awesome, respectful fear of God that you are supposed to have as a Christian, then falling into Satan's schemes and temptations will not be so easy. When we are afraid of God's power, discipline, and judgments as a loving parent's response to our sin, then we will avoid most sin like it was a disease that we would never want to become infected with.

"Hate what is evil; cling to what is good" (Romans 12:9). We need to hate evil, sin, and the Devil's schemes. We need to cling to God's word. It sounds pretty simple, and in reality it is. Superficial Christianity and a love for the world are what keep most of us from living out this verse the way it is written.

I hope this discussion has deepened or helped confirm part of your understanding about spiritual warfare. This chapter was not intended to build a fanciful or abnormal view of spiritual warfare, demons, Satan, or anything along those lines. We do not focus on this or become consumed by these areas of study. Remember the point of the Paige Patterson sermon.

Live with the reality that spiritual warfare does happen—and probably at a higher level than we realize. Open your fellow Christians' eyes to where Satan is attacking them in their lives.

Remember that God is in control and is more powerful than Satan—now and in the future.

CHAPTER 7

Truth Matters and Is for All Ages

Truth demands confrontation; loving confrontation, but
confrontation nevertheless."
—Francis Shaeffer

It sometimes saddens me to look around at my generation and to think of my kids and their generation and pose the question: *Who will be the ones that will raise their voices and declare truth to this generation and the generations to come?*

I can easily slip into despair, as I see the dwindling numbers of preachers, teachers, and Christians in general who unashamedly declare, live by, and would give their lives for biblical and Christian truth.

Are there still good Christian teachers, authors, and preachers out there today? Of course there are! I could not go into enough detail on how much Ravi Zacharias, Chuck Colson, James Dobson, David Jeremiah, Voddie Baucham, John MacArthur, Josh McDowell, Lee Strobel, Paul Washer, and other less-known, local pastors and men and women of God have influenced my life. There are great women teachers as well who have done much in women's ministry, such as Joni Erickson Tada, Beth Moore, and the women associated with Women of Faith conferences.

What concerns me, though, is whether there will be any to follow in their footsteps. Will Christians in my generation or my children's generation rise up to the task of being a voice of truth? I hope so, and I hope that some of you who are called by God into full-time ministry and are reading this book will answer that call.

Some of you might be thinking, *Why is this guy so worried about things like that? Won't God always raise up preachers, teachers, evangelists, and missionaries? Why even be concerned about it?*

It might concern me because the majority of Christians in the United States of America have a "me-first" mentality instead of a "God-first" mentality. I believe this results in hundreds of thousands of Christians never giving God the opportunity to call them into ministry positions. That is why we have thousands of pastor-less churches, pages and pages of missionary assignments that remain vacant, and millions of unbelievers who never hear the gospel from a fiery, vibrant speaker.

It also concerns me how many individuals reject a mind-set that might even allow them to be called into a ministry position. Whatever excuse a person uses, it is still just that, an excuse. You are deliberately saying no to the Creator of the Universe and the One who is supposed to be your God and King. You call yourself a "Christian," which most people say means "little Christ" or "Christ-follower." Where is the "following" part of this label if you never follow? When do you ever "take up your cross" if you only live for yourself? Where and when do you ever represent Jesus if you will not follow God's will for your life? Can you ever look anything like Jesus if you never sacrifice anything for Him?

Answer the call, and open up your heart, mind, and soul. Go wherever God tells you to go, and do whatever God tells you to do.

Now, I know that not everyone is called into full-time ministry, so please do not hear this as a demand that every Christian be in a leadership or career position in a church or some ministry. But everyone is called to do something for the kingdom of God. Whether it is witnessing, helping out in some role at your local church, or doing something else God may have for you to do, you need to step up and do it.

My other concern is the number of actual cowards in Christianity—especially cowards in Christian leadership positions. (I know we hit on this in the spiritual warfare chapter, but go with me on this.)

I was talking with a pastor friend just the other week, and the conversation we had confirmed a troubling phenomenon that is going on all across our country.

We were going over some fairly random things before a Sunday service where he had graciously given me the opportunity to speak. I began sharing how much I enjoy a hard-hitting, in-your-face sermon that is seldom heard from pulpits today. I told him how I had just heard, in person, one of my favorite pastors from Fort Worth, Texas, who did not "pull any punches" when preaching, and how much my whole family had enjoyed hearing that message.

As I was ending my comment, he interrupted, saying, "But what happens when the church hits back?" He laughed, but his face portrayed a scared, deer-in-the-headlights look. The next look that crossed his face was a silent questioning, as if he was waiting for me to answer the question and show how naïve and inexperienced I was. We finished our talk amicably, and I tried not to have a confused look on my face.

As we drove back to our home, I vented to my wife. "As a messenger of God, who cares what the church thinks about your message?" I remarked rather animatedly to her. She reminded me that many preachers probably couldn't really preach what they wanted to for fear of losing their jobs. That was when I was struck in my heart because, looking back at the prophets, Jesus, apostles, and early Christians, I see that they were not afraid to lose their *lives*, much less their jobs. It is cowardly and disgraceful that we would seek out the approval and worry about the opinions of mankind instead of being more worried about what God thinks of it.

Have we forgotten that teachers, evangelists, people in leadership, and pastors will be judged at a stricter level than others? I think that, besides judging them on shepherding, God will look at how well they delivered the message He gave them.

The heartbreaking thing is that most preachers, teachers, and others in leadership that I see in today's churches couldn't care less about what God wants them to talk about. They care more about being relevant. They want to be funny and have their messages accepted by all.

Or they sometimes fall to the other side, caring only about doing things the way they have "always been done." They care nothing about relevance and culture. They don't care that their church is dying, as long as they are happy.

It takes devotion to God, caring what He thinks, and knowing that you will be judged, to overcome these aspects. To avoid becoming a cowardly messenger of God, you have to fear the living God who created the universe and everything in it and believe that He actually wants you to say specific things at specific times. Believe that, and by the Holy Spirit, He can say things through you that will impact people on a supernatural, extraordinary, and divine level.

We have to preach God's Word. God's Word is not limited to grace, love, mercy, and forgiveness. You are committing a spiritual crime if you are a messenger of God in any capacity and you do not include topics such as God's wrath, justice, judgment, and holiness in your teachings. If you never challenge people to pursue righteousness, to live holy lives, to be concerned about sin, or to fear God, I wonder what Bible you are reading. It would be obvious that we are not reading the same Bible, unless you had intentionally ignored some passages or never read the Bible in its entirety in the first place.

I beg you not to be a superficial or "fake" messenger of God. If you are, my heart breaks for you on judgment day.

One last thing we need to remember about being heralds of truth while delivering God's message is this: Not everyone is going to like it. It might cost you your job. It might cost you your family. It might cost you your very life. This has happened since the beginning of time, and it will happen until Jesus finally sets things right.

Take what happened to Zechariah in 2 Chronicles 24:17-22, for example.

> After the death of Jehoiada, the officials of Judah came and paid homage to the king, and he listened to them. They abandoned the temple of the Lord, the God of their fathers, and worshiped Asherah poles and idols. Because of their guilt, God's anger came upon Judah and Jerusalem. Although the Lord sent prophets to the people to bring them back to him, and though they testified against them, they would not listen. Then the Spirit of God came upon

Zechariah son of Jehoiada the priest. He stood before the people and said, "This is what God says: 'Why do you disobey the Lord's commands? You will not prosper. Because you have forsaken the Lord, he has forsaken you.'" But they plotted against him, and by order of the king they stoned him to death in the courtyard of the Lord's temple. King Joash did not remember the kindness Zechariah's father Jehoiada had shown him but killed his son, who said as he lay dying, "May the Lord see this and call you to account."

From this passage, we see that Zechariah was not exactly rewarded kindly for delivering God's message to the people. He stood up and boldly proclaimed the truth to the people. Not only did they violently kill him by stoning him, but they killed him in the courtyard of God's temple. To put that into perspective today, we would say they killed him at church.

Some of you may think, "Thank goodness we don't live in those times." If you think that we do not treat messengers of God that way today, think again. We spiritually stone and kill messengers of God all across the United States. Preachers get fired for not speaking the kinds of messages congregations wants to hear, when instead those congregations should be broken and repentant because of the messages. Evangelists and revival speakers are never invited back, because they speak too much about people's sins, repentance, and God's judgment instead of focusing on God's love, grace, and forgiveness. Christian speakers are kicked out of conferences for citing Scripture in their sessions and for standing firm on biblical truth. The times we live in are sad, and it will take fortitude, courage, determination, and faithfulness to persevere as a messenger of God today.

I challenge you who are messengers of God to faithfully fulfill God's calling for your life and to deliver a message that will bring God's people back to Him if He gives you such a message. Do not be a coward and fail the living God and your Lord and Savior Jesus Christ.

Let's move on to some specific truths that the Lord has laid on my heart and that need to be heard.

Truth For You, Me, And Everyone Else

In these next sections, there will be arrows of truth flying around. They will either hit you where you are or where you have already been. Whether they are able to pierce your heart or not is up to you.

Youth and Youth Leaders

I was a hedonistic youth, rebellious in my later high school years, and a downright disgrace to my family name and the church I was raised in. I deliberately rejected the teaching, morals, ethics, and values that my family and church had spent generations passing down. I was the first to put a black smudge on my family name as a result of some of the choices I made. As much as I try now, some of the consequences and results from those decisions will never wash the stain off a family name that never had some of the problems or sins associated with it until I smeared it. I freely and ashamedly admit it.

The sad thing is that in present youth culture, most young people have no idea about right and wrong. They have no grasp of biblical ethics, morals, and values. Because of that, they couldn't care less about bringing honor to their name or their church family. For what does that have to do with their real pursuit? Their real pursuit is of money, status, fame, and any or every material thing that will make them happy.

Who is to blame for this tragedy that few even realize is going on? Past and present generations of adults!

These are adults who let the youth start meeting separately from the adults. Instead of caring about the church as a whole—and the importance of teens maturing and paying attention to the model of how "grown-ups" act—the focus turned to ways we could best serve the teenagers. This resulted in the hearts of the youth turning away from the hearts of their fathers, and this brings about serious consequences.

These are adults who care more about being relevant and cool with teenagers than about training them up and discipling them into adulthood. Instead of solid biblical wisdom, spoken and lived out in front of our youth today, we have fun and stuff, fluff and games. We have silly and sometimes very inappropriate games being played in youth groups all over this country. The maturity levels of the youth leader and the youth are sometimes the same.

Why do we not see a problem with this? Why do we look and laugh, when we should be appalled? Well-meaning adults will laugh and snicker while saying to each other, "Kids will be kids" or "That youth pastor sure is crazy, but at least he entertains the kids." What we really should realize is this: our youth are radically depraved and living in a viciously anti-God culture. We should be asking each other what we are doing to help prepare them for the horrific battles that are waiting for them when they leave their homes and try to live as adults.

In my short experience with youth and collegiate ministry, I have found that church people in general care more about how many people are at the meetings than about what is taught at the meetings. As long as the kids are coming and being entertained, there is a sense of victory, success, and a "vibrant" youth ministry. If, however, numbers start dwindling because you are actually teaching a hatred of sin and love for holiness and righteousness, and you start offending the fragile self-esteem of an adolescent because you confronted some ungodly thinking or actions, then you are failing at youth ministry and are informed that these things should not be taught in a modern youth group. Because of watered-down gospel teachings (if they are even "gospel" at all), fun-centered group meetings, and cowardly youth pastors, we have thousands upon thousands of youth that are going straight to hell, while all their churches happily do nothing to prevent it.

About a year ago, my wife and I started helping with a youth group at one of the largest churches in our city. They told us they already had enough helpers with organizing activities; they just needed somebody to speak to the group every Wednesday night. It was an offer I couldn't refuse. Not that I like to hear myself speak; I just love opening up the Word of God and speaking what God lays on my heart.

The first meeting we went to was a shocking experience, to say the least. The Scripture we were going to study that evening was about how Jesus is the Way, the Truth, and the Life. We only got to the part where Jesus was the Way. I thought I was only going to mention in passing that Jesus was the only way to heaven and that if you didn't believe in Him you would be choosing to go to hell. Little did I know that it would start a huge fight that would make us question if we should ever come back to that youth group again.

When I said that Jesus was the only way, I was interrupted by a senior girl in the group. (This angered me, because where I grew up, you interrupted the teacher at your own peril.) She emphatically told me how wrong I was to say that Jesus was the only way to heaven. When I challenged her to explain what the verse meant, she stumbled and stammered about how the verse probably meant what I was trying to say it meant.

Then in the same breath, she said something that chilled me to the bone, because she was supposedly a Christian. She said, "But that is not what is important. The important thing is a person's belief. If someone believes something, we cannot tell him he is wrong. As long as a person believes in God, he is okay; we shouldn't tell anyone what to believe, because everyone is going to heaven."

I let the discussion go on for a little while after that, because I was so shaken that a girl who seemed to be looked up to by her peers could say something so far from the truth. Relativism had definitely shaped her thinking. It was comforting that a fight started in the group, because some of the youth actually had a true understanding of Christianity and began a heated debate with the girl and a few others who joined her side. I quickly cut in and taught the rest of the lesson from a "historical" Christian viewpoint that silenced the opposition. Then we broke up into a boys' group and girls' group for more discussion, application, and prayer.

The guys' group went great. We had good discussion, the youth brought up a few application points that were good, and prayer time was glorifying to God. So I was surprised when my wife came out of the girls' meeting and was obviously emotionally upset.

She said that when another wife of a youth leader opened up the time for discussion about the lesson, fireworks started. The girl who had disagreed about Jesus being the only way immediately began griping about how insensitive I was. She went on to say that she wouldn't be coming back, if this was the way this youth group was going to go. The other wife and my wife stood firm on what the Bible truly teaches, and some other youth came alongside them. My wife said it ended with an awkward prayer and the girl leaving very quickly without speaking to anyone.

This story ends with us losing the girl who was so against biblical teaching, as well as a few others. We spent the rest of the year we were there pounding biblical truth into their brains. For most of the year, I felt like a failure. I would go home in an almost depressed state, because I felt like nothing was happening except the equivalent of talking to a fence post. Most of the time, it seemed like the kids couldn't care less about what we were talking about. Even the pastor's son was falling asleep during the lessons. I was so sad, because I knew that they were hearing what God wanted them to hear, but there was no fruit to show for the labor.

It was not until almost the end of our time there that God showed me something. We brought in a guest speaker who was great and was in-their-face with the truth. He taught on the importance of witnessing and emphasized that they were not doing their jobs at all if they were not involved in evangelizing their peers. He even went so far as to tell them they were failing as Christians if they were not witnessing to unbelieving close friends or family members. (Needless to say, I loved this guy.)

As I sat there listening to him speak, I felt God begin to speak into my heart. He told me to look around the room at the youth. I noticed that every eye was open, soaking in what he was saying, and some were being struck to the depths of their hearts by the message. I started tearing up—just like I am doing as I write this—because I personally never thought this would have been possible with such a rebellious and biblically ignorant youth group.

God told me that these kids used to be rocky and thorny ground that rejected the gospel and biblical messages, but our commitment to Him and His Word had changed that. Through continued, hard fighting against worldly thinking and "working the ground," so to speak—and with God's and the Holy Spirit's help—we had changed the unfertile ground to fertile ground.

While every head was nodding, and while they applauded the speaker after he was finished, I was trying to stop the tears from flowing. I had cried out to God after meetings throughout the year with no answer, only the assurance that I was speaking what He wanted me to. I wanted answers as to why they were not listening, and I wanted to stop feeling like a failure all the time. All those months of frustration and emotional turmoil washed away that night.

God finished by telling me that their acceptance of the message and the growth that was going to come from that night was possible because of what we had gone through to get them to that point. If we had not done all our hard work and teaching, they would have rejected the guest speaker's message and not even have paid attention to him. I couldn't wait to tell my wife what God had revealed to me, and when I did, we spent the rest of the night rejoicing and praising God.

How many youth leaders, youth, and speakers will get to go through what we went through? I hope thousands—if not millions. I really do. The sad truth is that probably not many will.

Because so few speakers are heralds of the truth and bold in their declarations, they will never see rocky soil turn into fertile soil.

Because so few youth see value in listening to, reading and applying, standing firm on, and committing their lives to the Word of God, they will never mature into strong Christians or see God's promises come true. They will not conquer the world, their community, or their family for Christ.

Because so few youth leaders actually follow God and truly lead their groups down the roads God wants them to go down, youth groups will never be where God intends for them to be.

Some Words to Teenagers Today

One of the things that kills me the most is the lack of respect and honor for parents among teenagers today. If you are a teen, pre-teen, or young adult, I hope you will read this section with an open heart and open mind. If some of the words sting, I hope that you will pray and change your heart. If some of the words break your heart, I hope you will look to God for Him to fix it.

You are commanded to honor your father and your mother, no *ifs*, *ands*, or *buts* about it. So why don't you? If you think they are not worthy of honor or respect, that thought in your mind is from Satan and is unbiblical!

In case you don't believe this, I would challenge you to look it up for yourself. Here are some of the references that deal with God commanding you to honor your parents: Exodus 20:12, Deuteronomy 5:16, Matthew 15:4-6, Matthew 19:19, Mark 7:10, Mark 10:19, Luke 18:20, and Ephesians 6:2.

As with any Scripture, read the words surrounding these verses for more understanding. I may not know much, but if God saw fit for certain words to come out of His own mouth, Jesus' mouth, and Paul's mouth in His Word, I think they might be important enough to pay attention to.

You may read those verses and say to me, "But you don't know my dad or my mom. If you knew them, you would know how awful, terrible, dumb, stupid, or evil they are."

If your parents are evil—and by that I mean if they have ever sexually or physically abused you, never taught you anything about Scripture or believing in Jesus Christ or God, or if there's another evil reason I am not thinking of—then you do have it pretty bad, and I pray that God delivers you from that situation somehow. It is up to Him whether that means getting you out of the situation or saving their souls and stopping them from whatever it is that they do against the will of God.

The point is still the same, though: you are supposed to honor and respect them, no matter how they treat you. It is not your fault if they are evil or ungodly; it is theirs. They will answer to God for how they treat you and how they have raised or trained you. Just remember that you will answer to God as well for how you honored, obeyed, showed respect, and took care of them in their latter years.

Some of you are blessed beyond imagination, because you are fortunate enough to have godly Christian parents. I hope that you stop reading this book right after this sentence, get down on your knees, and lift up a heartfelt prayer to God Almighty in thankfulness for giving you Christian parents. You do not realize how lucky you are. The majority of mankind does not have Christian parents, and many children all across the world would die to be in your shoes.

The sad thing is that most Christian kids I know bemoan their stations in life. They whine and cry because of how "stupid" their parents are. Just because your parents don't know how to run the newest iPad, computer, or some kind of game, that does not make them dumb. They do not have any less wisdom about God or His ways because of things like that.

Just take simple logic for a spin. Think back to how smart you were in kindergarten and then about how much knowledge you have gained in each year of your life that followed. Isn't it amazing to think how much knowledge and intelligence you gain every year of your life? Now ask yourself why you think that stops when a person get to be your parents' age.

It doesn't make much sense, does it? That's because you continue to get smarter every year. You continue to gain wisdom the longer you are on this planet. Even if you are committed to being a vegetable or a couch potato, over time you will become wiser about how to be a vegetable or couch potato. So, please, do not fall into the trap from Satan and start disrespecting and dishonoring your parents. God *hates* that.

Honoring, respecting, and obeying your parents will help you greatly in your Christian walk—and in your life in general. You will learn to respect and honor those in authority outside your home. This will lead to teachers and future employers seeing that you are different from most other young people in the world. The end result will be a tendency to receive better grades in college just because the professor enjoys your behavior more than the disrespectful students. When hundreds interview for a job and there are several applicants with the same credentials, an employer might just pick you when he remembers the respect and honor you showed him. You must remember that there are always rewards for obeying and following God's Word. It is my personal opinion that, whether it is in this life or in eternity, the rewards are great.

Eternal rewards will be bigger, better, and greater than we can imagine. I hope you, as a young man or young woman, will start to think about eternity in a very real and gripping way. If you died today or tomorrow, would God be happy with how you treated your parents?

Would He be happy with how you treated those in authority—whether at home, school, or church?

I beg you young people who are reading these words to take God and His Word seriously. Let them change your heart and your goals for this life. If you were lucky enough to grow up with Christian parents, do not abandon the way you were raised! Do not bring shame, dishonor, or disgrace to the name of the family you belong to. Do not bring shame, dishonor, or disgrace to the name of your Savior and Lord Jesus Christ! Stay on the narrow road that leads to life. Run from the temptations and lies of the broad road that leads to destruction.

Keep reading as well. If you feel convicted, you might find the words to parents and grandparents comforting, for now it is their turn.

Parents

This section is very personal to me. My wife and I are the proud parents of three children, and we are in the midst of trying to raise and train them to be authentic Christians. I never imagined that the life of a parent would be so challenging, heartbreaking, stressful, rewarding, fulfilling, joy-filled, and complex as it is. I hope you fellow parents will hear the words contained in this section as words coming from someone going through some of the same struggles you are, someone who is not a perfect parent, someone who is going through the refining fire to become a more godly parent, and someone who prays daily to God for insight, instruction, rebuke, correction, and wisdom in how to function as a Christian parent.

I say this to hopefully show you that I am not an arrogant know-it-all in this area. I am just a Christian father trying to live, think, feel, and behave the way a true Christian father should. If any of the following is convicting or challenging to you, I hope you will remember that it is just one Christian parent trying to point the way for other Christian parents to go.

"Fake" and immature Christian parents are ruining the lives of countless children, youth, and young adults across our country today. I see this when I talk to parents and listen to them lament over the struggles their kids are going through or how their kid has turned his or her heart away from God. When I ask them how their prayer time with their kids is going or how their kids respond to godly conversations or biblical instruction, they look at me as if I was a raving idiot. Excuses and sheepish looks abound, and they usually say something like this:

"Well, we just got busy, and we don't have time for that anymore."

"We've never really done that."

"What are you talking about? I said my kid is having problems. What do you suggest we do about it?"

Varying responses like the ones above have shocked me to my core. How can we aspire to be good Christian parents but never teach our children the truth found in God's Word? How can we expect our children to know how to pray if we do not show them how, if we do not tell them of prayers answered years ago and the ones answered last week? It makes me want to scream and hit people with my Bible (well, maybe not that bad, but probably) to see so many parents dumbfounded by why their children do not care about God when it is obvious that they have only a superficial interest in God themselves.

This reminds me of my first job as a counselor and a parent's rather volatile reaction to a counseling session. I had been counseling the teenage boy of a single mother for many weeks and thought I had a good grasp on the situation. He was skipping school, getting into fights, and had recently been apprehended by the police for putting graffiti all over some park bridges. Counseling was a last-ditch effort before sending the boy to a teenage detention center.

After a few sessions, the teenage boy opened up. I learned that he had a pretty bad home life. People on drugs stayed at his house frequently, his mother was an alcoholic, and he never knew if there would be a meal on the table. These were just some of the many problems he endured on a weekly basis. We managed to work on his personal responsibility and even batter down the hate he had for his mother. The next move,

I thought, would be to bring the mother in so we could work on some rather obvious family issues. Boy, was I wrong!

The mother arrived at the counseling session and was subdued at first. She listened as I reported on what we had gone over and the progress that had been made. When I was beginning to make the transition into her opinion on what he had said about the home life, she quickly interrupted. She filled me in on how her son was rebellious, hateful, and full of mischief, that he never listened, and that he was just an all-around "bad" kid. She went on and on, seemingly without any end in sight.

I tried in vain to get her to push all of that aside and just focus on what he was saying about their home life that bothered him. She jumped up and began to scream at me about how I didn't know anything about their life, how I had no right to talk about their "business," and how it didn't matter how she lived her life, because the problem was the kid and not anything to do with her. She stormed out with her son trailing along behind her. I never saw them again.

Sadly, this kind of family situation transfers all too well into the arena of being a Christian parent. Many times I have had the privilege of talking with youth and have then been introduced to their families. Some instances were times of crisis, and some were times where the parents just wanted to get to know the youth leader. It is amazing how quickly you can tell which families truly focus on God, His Word, and raising their children to be Christians while trying their best to live genuine Christian lives themselves.

It is also amazing how quickly you can tell which families are not raising their children to be genuine Christians. Their homes reek of materialism, disrespect, and worldly pursuits. "God is first" comes from their mouths, but a closer inspection reveals that to be only a superficial stutter. Sports, entertainment, activities, pursuit of money, and a job that will make them "happy" are really first in their homes. Then they wonder why their children never go to church again when they leave home.

If we raise our children in an anti-God culture, in an anti-God and anti-Bible thought process or education system, in a home that is devoid of any godly or biblical instruction, then it really shouldn't surprise us when they are drawn to an anti-God culture or anti-God and anti-Bible thought processes—and then raise their own children in a worse home, spiritually speaking, than they were raised in.

Where is the answer for all this? What comfort can we draw from Scripture? How about a verse that parents love to throw in my face, even when they are not raising their children up to be followers of Christ at all?

"Train a child in the way he should go, and when he is old he will not turn from it" (Proverbs 22:6).

I completely agree with that verse; I think I am living proof of that verse. The idea that gets thrown at me is that any parent who calls himself a Christian and takes his child at least one day out of the week to church is following that verse to the letter and has insurance that their child will turn out to be an "on-fire" Christian when they get older. I wish you could hear the howls of frustration in my mind when I am confronted with that kind of thinking. I want to yell, "Are you kidding me?"

If you agree with those parents and define "train" in that way, then you are dead wrong. If your child turns out to be a real, authentic, thriving, maturing, and true Christian after being raised that way, you will be lucky and have to thank God for His immeasurable grace, mercy, love, and forgiveness.

If you mean "train" by the standards of Deuteronomy 4-6 and the Proverbs that talk about raising and training children—and anywhere else in the Bible for that matter—then you are on the right path. It is the only path that will truly result in your child becoming a God-fearing Christian who is bold in his faith and full of faith, hope, and love for himself and others. This will require you to learn Scripture. This will require you to be open about your faith journey with your children. This will require that you be on your face, praying to God for every aspect of your child's life. This will require that you teach your child the ways of our God and our Savior Jesus Christ.

I can hear the cries of "This is too much! How can you expect me to do that in this day and age?" or "Oh, so you want me to become a Jesus Freak parent?" or "That wasn't the way I was raised, and I am a pretty good Christian, so I am definitely not going to all that trouble."

First of all, the things listed above are not "too much." They are only the basic ingredients of what it takes to be a real and authentic Christian parent that wants to pass along his faith to his children. Also, whenever you begin to think that anything in your Christian life is "too much," stop and remember what Jesus did for you. He left heaven, was obedient to God in everything, suffered more than we can imagine by his violent death and being forsaken by the Father, endured God's wrath being poured out on Him, and now sits at God's right hand as the High Priest and mediator for a very crooked and depraved Christian generation (of which I am foremost). That kind of thinking has the tendency to put us back into the right perspective.

Secondly, if you think that you can raise your kids exactly the same way your parents did, then you are only kidding yourselves. We are in the midst of the most ungodly, sin-filled, and dark times of the entire history of the United States of America. If you doubt this, then just visit www.foxnews.com, www.cnn.com, or even the dreaded www.msnbc. com. Take a look at the headlines, and try to keep your Christian soul from shuddering while you look at the horrific things going on all across our nation.

It reminds me of Isaiah 59:9: "So justice is far from us, and righteousness does not reach us. We look for light, but all is darkness; for brightness, but we walk in deep shadows."

Our culture, education system, court system, and most of politics are against anything to do with the Bible, God, and especially Jesus Christ. It is only going to get worse. We must prepare our children for the things that are coming. It would not be a great leap of the imagination to say that within our lifetimes, Christianity will become illegal in our country. For all the talk of "religious freedom," one day it will not be there for true followers of Christ.

How do we prepare them for this? Being open and honest is a good start. Read the verses in the Bible that talk about the end times. Tell your children how people will only listen to teachers who say what their itching ears want to hear, which is undeniably going on today. Make sure they know how the Holy Spirit will help us at times when we are dragged in front of police, judges, or anyone else to be put on trial for our faith. Teach them how to be the first ones to raise their hands and identify themselves as Christians, if the government troops or police ever kick in the door and ask, "Are you Christians?"

Talk with them about what has happened to Christians ever since Jesus died. Tell them how every disciple except John died a martyr's death. Read to them the accounts of first-century Christians and the emperors and kings who mercilessly hunted and burned them and then even herded them into sporting arenas to be killed by animals and gladiators. Tell them of such great Christian heroes as Perpetua, William Tyndale, John Bunyan, Richard Wurmbrand, and others who suffered, spent time in jail, or were tortured or killed for their belief in Jesus Christ and for following God's will for their lives.

You might think it's a little strange for me to be writing about this in the parenting section. I only write it to help you see what we will have to deal with in our lifetimes—and if not ours, I guarantee it will be within the lifetimes of our children. If they are not prepared for this, I fear that most will throw away their faith in Jesus Christ, in God, and in the Bible. I do not think all the blame will fall on them. It will fall on us as parents, because we did not prepare them for what was coming.

In closing, I would like to single out dads and moms because of what I see going on in many churches today across our country. On Father's Day and Mother's Day, we celebrate dads and moms. It is a wonderful time to show our appreciation for our fathers and mothers on their respective days. What makes my stomach turn is when the pastor gets up in front of a congregation on those special days and pours praise on every dad and every mom. Sometimes a pastor will preach out of Proverbs 31 and then talk about how glad he is that his church is full of that kind of woman. Or he might preach a sermon about dads, which usually never even has anything to do with how a father is supposed to be the spiritual head of the household. When this happens, I get righteous indignation and extremely nauseated.

Sorry, dads. Don't expect a pat on the back if you are not leading your families like you are commanded to do in Scripture. You are supposed to be the guide, the pacesetter, and the head of your family. You will answer to God for how you did in this area.

Unfortunately, too many Christian fathers have listened to feminism, TV sitcoms, and other influences and have already given up in this area of their lives. We are not the stupid and bumbling fools that most TV shows portray us to be. And if you are in that category, then *grow up!* Start taking your responsibilities seriously and lead your family from the darkness into the light. Read Ephesians 5:21-33 for a better understanding of this.

Now that you have read that, remember that we are not supposed to be tyrannical rulers of the house. We have a lot of work to do if we are going to love our wives the way God wants us to and if we are going to treat them like the gentle flowers they are and love them like Christ loved the church. Wow! That is the highest level of love there ever was and ever will be. Can we even begin to touch the depths of that kind of sacrificial, all-consuming, earth—and heaven-shaking love?

Love, honor, and cherish your wives. Lead your family well. Get a "Well done good and faithful dad!" when you get to heaven. Rearrange your priorities if you are not living this way, so you will not hear, "Foolish, evil, and lazy dad!" when you get to heaven.

Now it is the mom's turn. Being a Proverbs 31 woman is popular right now. My wife is presently carrying around a "31" bag, and has held thirty-one parties to help a friend who is selling that merchandise. It is supposed to point to being a Proverbs 31 woman. I think it is a great business and a wonderful witnessing opportunity.

Moms, just don't claim to be a Proverbs 31 woman if you do not exhibit any of those characteristics. Do not embarrass yourself by claiming to be a godly woman if you are full of sarcasm. Please do not think of yourself as this Proverbs woman if you are a high-maintenance woman, totally consumed by materialism and the way the world says women should be.

It is much easier to listen to a preacher tell you how great a mom you are than to actually read Proverbs 31 and be broken by it. If you have never read Proverbs 31, then please take the time to prayerfully read over it and apply it to your life. Oh, and read Ephesians 5:21-33 as well, so you can be on the same page as your husband.

You are commanded to be your husband's helpmate and encourager and to be respectful and submissive to him. I pray that you hear and read those words with godly understanding, especially when most women these days can't even hear the word *submission* without immediately going up in flames.

Just as husbands are not supposed to be lazy bums, wives "must" respect their husbands. Wives, you might be bristling right now and thinking, *But he does nothing worthy of respect.* If that is the sad truth in your marriage, then I pity you. But it is more likely that this world, your sinful nature, and Satan have deceived you into thinking that way and treating your husband without respect, and you are just used to your relationship being that way. It does not matter how your husband thinks or behaves, or what his bad habits are; you are called to respect him. In the same way, it does not matter how sarcastic or high-maintenance a wife is, or how many bad habits she has; the husband is called to love her. The focus is on you, not your spouse. Are you doing a good job of respecting your husband and submitting to his leadership? If not, then change your thoughts, actions, and feelings until you do.

This will be one of the best witnessing opportunities to your children. If Dad is someone who takes a serious role in leading the family spiritually, the children will take notice. If Dad is someone who pours love out on his wife, sons will turn out like him and daughters will look for a husband like him. If Mom is one who respects her husband, the children will have more respect and pride in their father. If Mom is truly a Proverbs 31 woman, people in the community and church will notice, the children will take pride in their mother, her home will lack nothing, and it will be a place that glorifies God.

I beg you, parents, to be truly godly parents that lead your children to righteousness and away from sin. If you are not doing any of the things talked about in this section, or if you couldn't care less about the aspects we've gone over, then you are failing as a Christian parent!

Please repent and turn back to God.

Grandparents

Just so no one can leave this section without being challenged or convicted, let's talk to you grandparents. You have a job and responsibility just like the youth and parents. Grand-parenting is not time for just playing, fun, and games.

That is what we would like to think, though, isn't it? For someone to be a good grandparent, all they have to do is pour on the love, praise, and spoiling, right?

I would propose to you that this kind of thinking is from the Devil. If all you do as a grandparent is have a Coke and a joke for your grandchildren, and all you tell them is how good they are, then I hope you can see the problems with that.

Where is the passing-down of the Christian legacy? Do you ever spend time with your grandchildren, explaining why you believe what you believe? Have you told them about your prayer life or about what prayers God has answered throughout your lifetime? Do they know what your favorite verses in the Bible are? Have you shared any part of your faith with them? If you have not done any of these things, then *why not?*

When I have had the privilege of counseling grandparents and we come to these questions, the most frequent answer is, "I'm afraid I might lose my relationship with them." Maybe you will—for a little while, or *you could be the one who helps draw them back into a right relationship with God.* You might be the only voice God can use that they will hear in this day and age.

Let me share a personal story. I was blessed to have two wonderful sets of grandparents. Both sets did a wonderful job of making sure we knew that they loved us. All four were Christians, but one set was different from the other. One set challenged me and ended up changing my spiritual walk with God forever, while the other never spoke of spiritual aspects with me, that I can remember.

It is sad to write this, because it breaks my heart. I knew they were Christians, and I knew they loved me, but today, as an adult who wants to pass on my Christian belief system to my children and grandchildren, I just wonder why they didn't do that. I wish I could go back and listen to them tell me what God did in their lives. I would give anything to hear their testimonies about how they came to faith in our Lord and Savior Jesus Christ. I've had to pray a lot about my attitude in this. I waver from being very sad to being angry about the whole situation when I think about it too much.

I would now like to tell the story about the other grandparents and how they changed the course of my life without even meaning to. My grandpa Jack loved God and Jesus as much as any man that has walked this earth. I remember the powerful way he prayed before mealtimes whenever we saw them. As I grew from a child into a young teen, I noticed how he loved to talk about God and the Bible. It seemed like he just couldn't help himself. I loved being around him, because he always had a smile on his face, and he always took the time to tell us stories of how he grew up and how times were much different then. He told stories of his own grandparents and what they were like, stories told with meaning and emotion.

During one visit, probably around a holiday, he spoke words to me that convicted me to my very core. It was at a time in my adolescent life when I was chasing girls and partying to my heart's content. I was sitting there, listening to Grandpa talk about something, when he started talking about our "Christian legacy." He went back through several generations of grandparents on both his mother's and father's sides of the family. He talked about who had carried the Christian legacy through. Sometimes it was only the husband, and sometimes only the wife—and sometimes both of them were strong Christians. He got to the present time and talked about how happy he was that both his children were Christians. Then he leaned forward, and with fire burning in his eyes he told me, "Don't let our Christian legacy die with you!"

I think he laughed after he said it, remarked about how he was talking too much, and asked me what was going on in my life. I mumbled something about how my life wasn't that interesting and asked him to tell me one of the stories that I had heard many times. While he launched into that story, I tried to put myself back together. He never knew how much he had broken me with that little challenge. I went home, knowing what I was doing was wrong, knowing that I needed to get back into a right relationship with God, and knowing that if I continued down the path I was on, the family Christian legacy would die with me.

It broke me into a thousand pieces, but at the same time it drew me back into a time of restoration with God.

I shudder to think what might have happened if he hadn't spoken those words to me. It wouldn't have been pretty, and I doubt I would be where I am in my walk with God if not for those words. I got to share that story at his funeral a few months back, and I challenged everyone at the funeral to live a real and genuine Christian life. My grandpa had asked me to really challenge people during his funeral and try to get them to rededicate their lives to Jesus Christ. And though he wasn't praising God with us at that moment, he would be dancing in heaven, because his funeral wasn't supposed to be about him but only about Jesus.

It is through tears that I think about his life and about how much he helped my wife and I while we were out on the mission field. I used to call him up, and sometimes he called me, and we just talked for long periods of time. He encouraged me and gave godly advice, the best he knew how. He always shared what was going on in his church and his Sunday school class and with the rest of the deacons at the church. He helped me through some dark times while I was in a period of depression, and he was always completely real, open, honest, and transparent in his discussions with me.

He told of times when he doubted God and about how the Lord had led him through those times. He didn't sugarcoat anything involving God, His Word, or the struggles we have as Christians. He always wanted me to "preach" to him as well. He told me that I was real and genuine and said how much he liked that. He told me to never let anyone change the way I talked or preached about God's Word, because not many people talked like I did anymore. He always ended every phone conversation and physical meeting near the end of his life with "Preach the Word." It was a challenge and a reminder to never get away from God's Word and the gospel.

I love him and miss him terribly. I also realize how blessed I was to have a grandfather like that. In talking to my grandmother at her house after the funeral, I realized how truly blessed I was to have her as a grandmother as well. She shared how much she missed him, but when we started talking about their Christian marriage together, she said something that astounded me. She said, "I felt called-on very early in our marriage to just help your grandpa wherever and in whatever he was going to do in life. I just made sure that I did all I could to help him do all that God wanted him to do."

As that sank in on the way home, my opinion of my grandmother soared to new heights. I had never known her that well because I had always been talking to grandpa, and grandma was kind of quiet, always behind the scenes. It took a little shine off my awe of grandpa when I realized what a great, godly woman he'd had as a helpmate.

I share these stories to show you grandparents what an awesome impact you can make on your grandchildren. It doesn't matter whether they are perfect, godly Christians or unbelieving heathens. You should be able to share your faith with them unashamedly and without fear. You can be as transparent as you want to be about your faith journey and how God has helped you through anything He has. Follow the Holy Spirit's guiding, watch how seeds are planted and faith is grown, and notice the results you get. If nothing happens, pray until you go to join our Lord in heaven. Maybe when you are reunited with your grandchildren in eternity, you'll get to hear about how God used your life and your words in their lives.

If you do none of the things suggested, or you couldn't care less about what was written in this whole "grandparent section," then you are failing as a Christian grandparent! I wouldn't want to be in your shoes on judgment day, and I am heartbroken for your grandchildren, that they do not have godly grandparents. They have grandparents who obviously care more about themselves than about passing on a godly Christian legacy.

Here are some helpful verses for youth, parents, and grandparents:

> "Honor your father and your mother, so that you may live long in the land the Lord your God is giving you" (Exodus 20:12).

> "Children, obey your parents in the Lord, for this is right. Honor your father and mother—which is the first commandment with a promise—that it may go well with you and that you may enjoy long life on the earth. Fathers, do not exasperate your children; instead, bring them up

in the training and instruction of the Lord" (Ephesians 6:1-4).

"He who fears the Lord has a secure fortress, and for his children it will be a refuge" (Proverbs 14:26).

"To have a fool for a son brings grief; there is no joy for the father of a fool" (Proverbs 17:21).

"A foolish son is his father's ruin, and a quarrelsome wife is like a constant dripping" (Proverbs 19:13).

"Discipline your son, for in that there is hope; do not be a willing party to his death" (Proverbs 19:18).

"Do not withhold discipline from a child; if you punish him with the rod, he will not die" (Proverbs 23:13).

"The rod of correction imparts wisdom, but a child left to himself disgraces his mother" (Proverbs 29:15).

"Discipline your son, and he will give you peace; he will bring delight to your soul" (Proverbs 29:17).

"A wife of noble character who can find? She is worth far more than rubies" (Proverbs 31:10).

"She speaks with wisdom, and faithful instruction is on her tongue" (Proverbs 31:26).

"Charm is deceptive, and beauty is fleeting; but a woman who fears the Lord is to be praised" (Proverbs 31:30).

"O my people, hear my teaching; listen to the words of my mouth. I will open my mouth in parables, I will utter hidden things, things from of old—what we have heard and known, what our fathers have told us. We will not hide them from their children; we will tell the next generation the praiseworthy deeds of the Lord, his power, and the wonders he has done. He decreed statutes for Jacob and established the law in Israel, which he commanded our forefathers to teach their children, so the next generation would know them, even the children yet to be born, and they in turn would tell their children. Then they would put their trust in God and would not forget his deeds but would keep his commands. They would not be like their forefathers—a stubborn and rebellious generation, whose hearts were not loyal to God, whose spirits were not faithful to him" (Psalm 78:1-8).

"Is this the way you repay the Lord, O foolish and unwise people? Is he not your Father, your Creator, who made and formed you? Remember the days of old; consider the generations long past. Ask your father and he will tell you, your elders, and they will explain to you" (Deuteronomy 32:6-7).

"Only be careful, and watch yourselves closely so that you do not forget the things your eyes have seen or let them slip from your heart as long as you live. Teach them to your children and to their children after them" (Deuteronomy 4:9).

"These commandments that I give you today are to be upon your hearts. Impress them on your children. Talk about them when you sit at home and when you walk along the road, when you lie down and when you get up" (Deuteronomy 6:6-7).

Should we have these verses written on our hearts? Yes.
Should they shape and be the foundation for our thoughts, feelings, and actions as youth, parents, and grandparents? Yes.

If these verses are foreign to you or are not already on your heart, then a more troubling question would be, *Why not?*

In closing this chapter on truth and its paramount importance in so many areas of our lives, I would like you to take a look at yourself.

- Where does God's truth need to impact and change my life as a youth, a parent, or a grandparent?

- How can I apply what God has shown me through this chapter or in my spiritual walk this week?

- Did I just give superficial answers that I don't really intend to following through on? If so, I need to repent and come up with some deep thought—and prayer-filled answers!

You can do these things. Have a little faith that God wants to help you through this. Seek God in prayer. Find godly counselors and leaders to help you in any of these areas where you may not have a clue about how to change what God is telling you to change.

Have faith that God's truth is for our good, even when it hurts. Have faith that His Word will not lead you astray.

Afterword

It is with great joy and relief that we have finally come to this part. Honestly, I never thought it would come. I readily agree with something Dr. David Jeremiah said on the radio the other day when he was talking about his newest book. He remarked, "Someone asked me the other day if it was a joy to write a book. I replied that it was a joy to finish a book."

This has been the hardest thing I have ever done in my life. I have never been as emotionally, physically, and spiritually worn-out as I have been while laboring over this book. But looking back over the experience, I hear God saying, "See, that wasn't so bad, was it?"—with love in His voice, reminding me how big a baby I am at times. Excuse me while I laugh and cry at the same time.

I hope this has been a joy to you, the reader, as well. I pray that it has challenged you in areas where you are not living up to God's standards in your life. I hope that it has confirmed areas where you are. As a result, I pray that your faith will grow and become more steadfast, that you will live out a genuine and real Christian life that shines brightly for all to see, and that love, sacrifice, brokenness, holiness, righteousness, and contentment will overflow from your life to others around you.

The last verses I want to share with you are found in 2 Peter 1:5-9.

> For this very reason, make every effort to add to your
> faith goodness; and to goodness, knowledge; and to
> knowledge, self-control; and to self-control, perseverance;
> and to perseverance, godliness; and to godliness, brotherly
> kindness; and to brotherly kindness, love.
>
> For if you possess these qualities in increasing
> measure, they will keep you from being ineffective and
> unproductive in your knowledge of our Lord Jesus Christ.
> But if anyone does not have them, he is nearsighted and
> blind, and has forgotten that he has been cleansed from
> his past sins.

It is very clear to me that God tells us throughout the Bible that there is a way to live that pleases Him, and there are ways to live that do not. You can either live a genuine, authentic, real, and thriving Christian life, or you can live as a nearsighted and blind Christian, having forgotten the most important aspect of your life.

It is up to you and me to embrace a "radical" Christian life, which is really what God considers a normal one. It looks radical to others because they have so little faith—and because they either don't know or don't feel the need to grow.

Please change your life if need be, so it will honor our Lord Jesus Christ. Please follow Him wherever He tells you to go. Please carry your cross. Please pass on a Christian legacy to your family and to others you come in contact with.

Can we do anything else if we are truly Christ-followers? Can we seriously be satisfied with a life that is anything less than completely sold-out to Him? I hope not.

If you are only thirsting and hungering for the lusts of your eyes and of this world—whether it is materialism, sex, addiction, or living for the supremacy of yourself—please stop calling yourself a Christian. Do not drag the name of Jesus Christ, who is my Savior and King, through the mud and filth any longer. He does not deserve it, and it is no laughing matter.

It is a serious thing to play lightly with eternal matters and to anger the One who will judge everyone for everything they have ever done, whether good or bad.

My hope is that God and Jesus Christ are most important in your life. If, before you read this book, they were not, I hope that His will, His Word, and spiritual disciplines are the highest priorities in your life now. If not, reread this book or—infinitely more important—start reading your Bible every day. Ask God to make Himself known and real to you as you read. He will not let you down. Don't let Him down, either, through unbelief, lack of faith, or lack of understanding.

Don't be a "fake" or superficial Christian. Be one that is *ALIVE!*

CPSIA information can be obtained at www.ICGtesting.com
Printed in the USA
BVOW012244160212

283136BV00001B/6/P